*The American Novel and
the Way We Live Now*

BOOKS BY JOHN W. ALDRIDGE

Literary criticism

>   After the Lost Generation
>   In Search of Heresy
>   Time to Murder and Create
>   The Devil in the Fire
>   The American Novel and
>   the Way We Live Now

Fiction

>   The Party at Cranton

Social commentary

>   In the Country of the Young

Edited works

>   Critiques and Essays on Modern Fiction
>   Discovery #1
>   Selected Stories by P. G. Wodehouse

The American Novel and the Way We Live Now

JOHN W. ALDRIDGE

New York   Oxford
OXFORD UNIVERSITY PRESS
1983

Library of Congress Cataloging in Publication Data

Aldridge, John W.
The American novel and the way we live now.

Includes index.
1. American fiction—20th century—History and
criticism.   2. United States—Social life and
customs—20th century.   I. Title.
PS379.A515   1983   813'.54'09   82-7992
ISBN 0-19-503198-9

For Patricia and Ann

Portions of this book have been previously published,
usually in quite different form, in *Commentary,
Harper's, Saturday Review,* and the *Chicago Tribune
Book World.* I wish to thank the editors for permis-
sion to reprint them here.

I also owe a debt to the Rockefeller Foundation for
a Humanities Fellowship, which provided me with the
subsidy and time to complete a fair portion of the
writing.

Printing (last digit): 9 8 7 6 5 4 3 2 1

Printed in the United States of America

PREFACE

This book is at once a study, a commentary, and a meditation. It is a study—highly selective to be sure—of certain prominent features of the contemporary American novel. It is a commentary —highly subjective to be sure—on certain prominent features of contemporary American life. And it is a meditation on the possible connection between the two, the state of the novel and the character of the life.

Perhaps no responsible critic any longer takes seriously the old idea that the novel at any given moment in history can be considered a dependable fictive representation of the way of life prevailing at that moment—the suggestion made by Stendhal and others before and after him that the novel is a mirror carried along a high road or dawdling idly down a lane. The expectation that the novel will realistically reflect the experience of its time is not only fatigued, but has gone conspicuously unfulfilled, at least in this country, for a good many years. Most of our novelists now disdain the realistic reflection of life with as much vehemence as they disdain the happy ending. Indeed, their happiness seems most often to consist in the avoidance of endings, happy or otherwise, altogether and in perpetrating the most heretical violations of what once could confidently be thought of as the sacred law of verisimilitude. The contemporary American novel is perhaps most notable for its strong anti-realistic bias, and the surest way for any novelist to open himself to contempt is to resist that bias and create characters who bear some close resemblance to people one might encounter in ordinary daily life. He may comfort himself with the knowledge that he will probably be read by millions of grateful readers, but he will surely be snubbed by the critics and by his peers as meretricious and third rate.

And yet some relationship does exist, however remote and tangential it may be, between the material of the novel and the experience of the life from which, however indirectly, it derives. If nothing else, certain attitudes and unconscious assumptions, certain psychic styles and modes of perceiving reality that may be implicit in the life will be communicated or adumbrated in the fiction. For life is, after all, where the novel starts from, even though it may end at the remotest and most fantastic remove from what is conventionally recognized as life. The possibility that such a relationship exists has intrigued me for a long time, and anyone acquainted with my previous critical books will have seen that my tendency is to treat literature in its social and historical context. However unfashionable that approach may now be, I seem by temperament to be saddled with it and have no choice but to let it take me where it will.

With regard to any book purporting to discuss contemporary fiction, the question of the principle governing the materials selected for discussion always arises and is seldom answered to the complete satisfaction of those who raise it. I have chosen here to discuss materials that seem to me particularly illustrative of certain defining characteristics of our current fiction, and I have *not* intended to present a thorough or systematic survey of the best or most prominent works in the field. Such a survey of a subject so rich and varied would be an endless and probably foolhardy undertaking. But in any case, I have not undertaken it and do not wish to be haled into court for not having undertaken it.

I am also confronted with the problem that in earlier critical books I have said what I had to say about certain writers and now have no desire to recapitulate opinions that may have been better stated in those books. I have, therefore, refrained from discussing here the work of John Updike, John Cheever, Mary McCarthy, James Jones, Eudora Welty, Wright Morris, Truman Capote, and Gore Vidal—to name a few of the writers I might be faulted for not discussing—and hope that readers curious to know what my views of these and some other contemporary writers are or were will be led to read my earlier assessments of them, specifically in *After the Lost Generation, In Search of Heresy, Time To Murder and Create,* and *The Devil in the Fire.*

I am glad to say that the tendency of recent criticism is toward the subjective and impressionistic after decades during which it was virtually a matter of canonical edict that the critic should be invisible and the work be treated with the detachment of a biologist examining a specimen under a microscope. Some of our most sophisticated critics are now even going so far as to argue that the critic is the real and final maker of the work he criticizes, that his "reading" is far more crucial to the attainment of its ultimate significance than anything contributed by the mere author. I would not pretend to be quite so imperial in my claims. Still, it is pleasant to know that one is again permitted to be personal and provisional and conjectural and even crotchety and ironical without needing to feel embarrassed.

J. W. A.
Ann Arbor, Michigan
July 1982

CONTENTS

CHAPTER I

The Novel and the Imperial Self

Not the least of the effects of industrialism is that we become mechanized in mind, and consequently attempt to provide solutions in terms of engineering, for problems which are essentially problems of life.

T.S. Eliot

Preoccupation with the state of the novel was until about ten years ago one of the major bores of American criticism. From the early fifties well into the sixties it was scarcely possible to get through a month without reading—as a rule in the Sunday book review supplements or the editorial pages of *Life*—that the novel in this country was dying, was dead, was coming back from the dead, was being reincarnated in the mutant forms of a new journalism or a fictional nonfiction. Then quite suddenly the autopsical discussions stopped. And even though at this time in the criticism of the other arts such problems as the desperate plight of the theatre, the scarcity of talented new playwrights, the vacuity or vulgarity of current films, the faddishness of modern painting continue to be dissected with undiminished vigor, we very seldom hear anything more about the state of the novel, sick or well—presumably because we no longer care very much whether it lives or dies.

For those of us who have worked closely with contemporary fiction and may even be numbered among its more obsessive diagnosticians, an explanation for this rather curious development comes easily to mind, although a convincing explanation of the explanation may be enormously difficult to discover. Clearly, if public and critical interest in the novel has declined, it has done so in large part because the novel over the past decade has dramatically lost authority both as an art form and as an instrument for reflecting and educating public consciousness. We have long taken it for granted that the great innovative authority of the classic modern novel is now an entombed, even ossified authority represented by a body of sacred writings worshipped for their ancient wisdom and their ability to evoke the spirit of a dead historical past. But what still seems surprising, no matter how long we have lived with the fact, is that novelists we continue to think of as very much alive and functioning contemporaries have been similarly institutionalized, as if they were already considered as passé as their great predecessors, and have come to be admired more for their artistry than for their power to excite our imaginations or to deepen our understanding of the meaning of present-day experience. However gifted Bellow, Barth, Pynchon, Mailer, Roth, Heller, Updike, Hawkes, Gaddis, and our other important novelists may be, we somehow do not look to them for intellectual and imaginative leadership, as at one time we looked to the major novelists of the twenties and thirties.

Nor, for that matter, do we regard them as beings who, because of the originality of their work, have fascination as personalities or are leading lives that might in various ways instruct us in the possibilities of freedom, adventure, or individual integrity. Except for the two or three mostly third-rate novelists whose talent for self-caricature and bitchery has endeared them to talk-show audiences who know nothing of their books, the best of our writers today are ignored by the popular media unless and until they are arrested for disturbing the peace or manage to win the Nobel Prize. It is inconceivable that there is a novelist among us at this time who would be met by reporters at Kennedy Airport as Fitzgerald, Hemingway, even writers like Louis Bromfield and Pearl Buck, used regularly to be met when their ships arrived in New York from Europe.

It is also significant that the members of the current establishment of novelists are now all past forty-five and have produced very few highly talented descendants, even though they themselves had begun to appear with promising work in most cases by the time they were thirty. This would seem to suggest that the novel has not only lost authority but is failing, perhaps for just that reason, to attract the kind of new talent that might ultimately reconstitute its authority.

We may pass over the more obvious and cliché reasons why these things are so: how artists of all kinds have lost celebrity status in a time when only regular media appearance can, however temporarily, confer such status; how the novel has declined in influence with the decline in the habit of serious reading and with the rise of the dictatorship now exercised by television over the limited powers of mass public attention. These are factors we may cite without engaging the more complex realities of the problem. It is much more to the point to suggest that the authority of the novel never has been and probably never can be viewed as separable from the nature and quality of the human experience which, at any historical moment, may form its central subject matter. It is even possible that the novel will be most deeply influential at those moments when it is able to explore areas of experience that are not yet completely familiar to the reading public, thus functioning in its classic role as literally a bringer of the news, a discoverer of what is indeed novel.

These moments will usually coincide with periods of profound social dislocation, such as the rise of the mercantile middle class out of the collapsing order of feudalism—a process in which the novel as we know it in fact began—or they may be typified by radical changes in manners and morals of the kind that tend to follow major wars. They may also occur during the emergence of ethnic, racial, regional, and sexual subcultures in which the initial struggle out of feudalism of the middle class is recapitulated in the struggle for freedom, acceptance, and personal

autonomy of Jews, Blacks, provincial Southerners or Midwestern-
ers, women, or homosexuals—groups, in short, that have become
newly conscious of themselves and the special nature of their
minority or regional experiences.

Such central social transformations have over the past century
provided the American novel with a continuously replenishing
supply of vital materials, and always their vitality has depended
in very large measure on the factor of novelty, the opportunity
afforded novelists by historical accident to express for the first
time hitherto unknown or unexplored modes of feeling and
being, new experiences that in some ultimate way were working
to reshape the character of our national life and in the process
were introducing fresh perspectives from which to envision the
individual in some significantly altered relation to that life.
These experiences will of course have been shared by some
perhaps substantial part of the reading public. But they will not
have been made understandable or imaginatively available to
the public until recreated and evaluated in the work of an
important novelist.

The history of the twentieth-century novel in this country
may in fact be described as an evolutionary development in
which each successive generation of novelists has discovered and
appropriated to its particular creative use one or more of the
emerging social situations of its age, then has gradually—or in
some cases very quickly—depleted it of its potential as imaginative material, in time, as a rule, with its absorption into the
homogenizing system of the established national community.
There seems always to be a moment when a nascent subculture,
whether racial, ethnic, regional, or sexual, is, because of its
newness or its bizarre character, a particularly fertile ground for
the novel, just as there comes a moment when its materials will
have grown familiar to the point of becoming unusable clichés
and will lose authority to a more recently emerged subculture
possessing newer and as yet unfamiliar materials.

This is a major reason why it is possible to speak of the stages
in the growth of the American novel in terms of geographical
locale and minority-group interest—and the process has repeatedly involved the conquest, consolidation, and finally the

depletion and abandonment of new territories of social and imaginative experience. Beginning early in the nineteenth century and continuing through the years following World War II we have had the New England novel of Hawthorne and Melville; the novel of the developing Western frontier of James Fenimore Cooper; the more deeply Western novel of Mark Twain; the international and New York novel of James and Wharton; the many works appearing after the turn of this century that dramatized the plight of the Midwestern and Southern adolescent struggling to escape the suffocations of the small town; other works that explored the usually destructive consequences of the adolescent's escape—to New York, Long Island, Paris, and the south of France. Later during the thirties there were the large numbers of novels having to do with the new Depression-created subculture of the economically dispossessed.

After World War II the racial and ethnic novel came into authority as the Anglo-Saxon Midwestern experience ceased to be the typifying experience of most American writers. During that same period the Southern renaissance, initiated by Faulkner, reached maturity in the work of several writers who were among the last to derive their primary materials from geographical locale, materials which in their case were ultimately devitalized as a result of the proliferation of novels composed of self-parodistic Southernesque formulations. Currently, the best of our novelists seem, for reasons later to be discussed, to have turned away from the direct presentation of regional and subcultural experience, leaving the field largely to the newer women writers who, now that the homosexuals have had their day, are speaking for what may well be the sole remaining American subculture still capable of providing relatively fresh materials for the novel.

An obsessive hunger for new experience and a disposition to seek it in the actualities of the social world rather than to produce it imaginatively—these have been highly visible characteristics of our writers for as long as we have had a distinctively national literature. But what is perhaps less evident is how often their pursuit of novelty in material is joined with a preoccupation with the pursuit and exploration of novelty as a literary theme. If in the traditional European novel, characters tend to move in an environment already discovered and subdued by law, class hierarchy, and established custom, experience for Americans is an entity actively sought as destination and quarry, a dynamic and elusive state of both being and perpetual becoming that needs to be tracked down, grappled with, and brought under the control of the will and imagination. By the same token, dramatic conflict in the European novel has classically been generated within the givens of the established culture. Hell is indeed other people and the institutions they have created to force individual needs into harmony with communal interests, whereas the resolution of conflict is most often attained through the achievement of some more or less satisfactory mediation between individual and community. So the European novel again and again comes to rest in serenity and reconciliation, reminding us that salvation may perhaps be found only in an enlightened and usually chastened realignment of personal desire with public necessity.

The American novel tends by contrast to remain in a state of uncompromised adversary motion. Its characters move on or walk out at the end rather than regain admission to the social fold. The thrust of our imagination is resolutely kinetic, and the driving impulse is to seek salvation in escape from community and the confrontation of unknown possibility. It is not surprising that we have come to endow the search for new experience with mystical and sacramental meaning. To leave behind the known and, because known, commonplace reality is to invest in the promise of finding an elsewhere that will provide a second chance for being and consciousness, a regeneration of sensibility in the discovery of the authentic sources of the self. Cooper's intrepid and simple-minded frontiersmen, Melville's sea-going pioneers, Hemingway's seekers after the holy communion of precise language and true emotion, Fitzgerald's oddly ascetic sentimentalists of wealth and glamor—all are fantasy projections of an essentially religious view of experience, a belief in the possibility of some form of beatific transcendence to be achieved through submersion in elemental nature, the exploration of instinctual truth, or the discovery of an earthly paradise of infinite richness and perfect beauty. It would seem that the experience of the frontier along with its attendant myths founded on such ideas as that the corruptions of civilization can be left behind, that there exist inexhaustible territories of fresh challenge and adventure to be conquered, that the meaningful life is a continuous romantic pilgrimage into the virgin un-known, and that man is most noble as a pilgrim in the wilderness and closest to God when he is closest to nature— these have all obviously done much to program our psychic expectations just as they have helped to form a central thematic preoccupation of our novels.

But there has also been a contrary impulse at work behind the American novelistic imagination, and it may well derive from what remains of the original function of the novel as a form, which was to provide critical and satirical commentary on the excesses of the medieval romance. For even as our novels have expressed, and often seemed to celebrate, our romantic fantasies and aspirations to transcendence, they have also served—as a rule through the indirections of irony, metaphor, and ambiguity —as stern moral monitors of them. If there was a strong mythic and mythologizing dimension to the frontier experience, there was also an even stronger dimension of practical reality, physical hardship, privation, and danger—the inescapable limitations imposed by the environment upon the flights of the pioneer imagination. The conquest of the wilderness may have depended upon the existence of the dream of an earthly paradise, but survival in the wilderness depended upon the development of a hardy and altogether disenchanted pragmatism. Americans, we know, have never been at ease with the schizophrenia thus induced in them, and many of our most important novels have recorded with powerful intensity the anguish and frustration it has caused.

From the first genuinely American fiction of Cooper through the fables of Vonnegut, the pattern has repeatedly been one in which romantic aspiration or a certain idealistic vision of reality is subjected to the test of experience and shown to be empty pretense or illusion, founded on false values or meretricious hopes rather than on premises that take into account the practical necessities and the frailties of the human condition. The Ur-figures are of course Cooper's Leatherstocking and Melville's Ahab, both of whom are men obsessed with an idea of godliness and personal purity, and who pursue it in the conquest of, or escape into, the sanctity of nature. Leatherstocking is overtaken and finally destroyed by the evils of the civilization he was presumptuous and innocent enough to try to flee, while Ahab presumes beyond the limits of human power and is defeated by a force that is both natural and cosmic. Twain and James were both champions of the natural moral sense, that innate power of knowing right from wrong, which Thomas Jefferson believed to be part of the common property of all mankind. But both writers also knew that such a sense is a fragile weapon for survival in a world in which the universal possession of this sense is, in actual fact, proven again and again to be itself an illusion. In Twain's case it is the adult world into which one day Huck and Tom, like Holden Caulfield, will have to grow up. For James the continuing metaphor is the society of Europe in which Isabel Archer's and Lambert Strether's trusting American ingenuousness is educated into a sullied comprehension of the nature of evil and the necessity for personal responsibility. The emphasis in Fitzgerald is not dissimilar. Gatsby's virginity of heart, oddly augmented by the illegality of his business enterprises, is despoiled by the greater because morally lawless power of the Buchanans' carelessness and cynicism, their better understanding of the expedient ways of the world. In Faulkner a society basing its vision of itself on certain assumptions about a half-mythic, half-actual heritage of honor and nobility is overcome by the barbarous, wholly pragmatic Snopeses and their ilk, even as it is eaten away from within by false pride, blood guilt, and decades of duplicity perpetrated in the name of honor.

The list could be extended, but significantly enough, appropriate examples become scarcer as we approach closer to the present time. While it is true that the twentieth century has been remarkable for the accelerating vengeance with which novelists throughout the world have carried on the process of demythifying experience and eviscerating our illusions, it seems also to be true that at some point the dialectical balance had radically shifted. For we now suffer from a surfeit of negation and an apparent failure of understanding of just what values have been negated, what were the illusions we once mistook for truth, and what, if any, remain to be exposed. In a time when there is much evidence to indicate that fresh areas of social experience for the novel's exploration have sharply diminished in number, we must also confront the fact that the great demythifying function of the novel seems to have come to an end in a cultural situation in which there seems to be little of importance left to demythify and which has actually been engaged for years in a self-destructive process of demythifying itself. In almost every sector of human experience and endeavor—in politics, education, business, sexuality, marriage, the having and rearing of children—contemporary American society is itself performing the job once performed by our novelists, stripping away layers of idealistic assumption, hypocrisy, illusions of purpose, meaning, integrity, principle, and responsibility and exposing the emptiness or the corruption or the insanity beneath.

This has of course profoundly affected the nature of life in America at this time, hence, inevitably, the nature of the contemporary novel and our response to it. For if we once found pleasure, instruction, even perhaps a form of Aristotelian purgation of the emotions of pity and fear through seeing, in so many novels of the past, our idealistic aspirations subjected to the test of actuality and exposed as mistaken or illusory, we did so in part because aspiration in its conflict with actuality was endowed with virtue, even when affirmed in the face of hopeless odds. The urge for self-transcendence in the struggle to defend some abstract ideal of dignity, moral principle, or social responsibility was revealed as a response to some deep necessity within the human spirit, a hubristic challenge to the power of the gods in which defeat was finally the measure of the significance, even the tragic heroism, of that necessity.

Today, in most of the novels that, for artistic reasons, should be able to make a serious claim upon our attention, we find reflected a complex of conditions and responses of a radically different order. To the extent that they contain any realistic portrait of present actualities, they tend to dramatize not our hopes, but our feelings of generalized frustration and disappointment, not our need for transcendence, but our paranoid fears that some obscure force, some metaphysical CIA has robbed us of the means and the possibility and is bent on manipulating us in directions and for reasons we cannot understand and that have nothing to do with us personally. In fact, it is a characteristic feature of some of our best and most serious fiction that in it both the ideal and the reality of individual self-discovery and transcendence as central thematic preoccupations have been replaced by a dark fantasy in which prophecy and paranoia join to project a horror of universal conspiracy and mass apocalypse. At the center of that fantasy one discovers once again the classic modernist representation of the human condition: the dislocated self no longer sustained by the social structures and idealistic assumptions of the past, trapped in a demythologized and therefore demoralized present, dying a little more each day as the forces of entropy deepen and accelerate throughout the world. This is not a vision capable of giving us very much further instruction. Its meaning has been canceled by the cliché it has become, and it has lost its former adversary function: it is no longer a heretical corrective of the pieties behind our illusions. But it is, nonetheless, a reflection, however oblique and metaphorical, of a state of mind and condition of life we recognize as common now, even as we also recognize that one of the most frustrating features of our time is precisely that the vision of apocalypse, a relic of another age and so thoroughly devitalized by excessive literary use, should still have such pertinence to us. Yet there can be no question but that the conditions of which that vision was initially the radical expression have become more visible and seemingly more malevolent in our own age. We have, in fact, institutionalized all the famous old disaster syndromes and so assimilated them into our way of life and patterns of thought that disaster has become not only our central preoccupying experience, but our principal fantasy of salvation. If religions of the past offered promise of some form of transcendental redemption, disaster holds out the possibility of infinite and deliciously horrible forms of damnation, the ultimate titillation to orgasm of world holocaust, which in our ultimate boredom is one of the very few experiences left that is likely to bring us to feeling.

We now take it for granted—and the fact creates around us a subliminal envelope of rehabilitating drama—that we inhabit a world in which violence of any and every kind can erupt anywhere and everywhere at any time with or without provocation or meaning. This is a world that some few of us experience every day, but for the rest of us it exists as an abstraction projected and often seemingly created by the reality-manufacturing and reality-fantasizing media of television and film. Our direct experience is usually of another kind of abstraction, an urban or suburban non-community in which we are perhaps most conscious of floating in disconnection between business and home, passing and being passed by strangers in the void. Home is the place of brief refuge from the void, where family offers a substitute for community even as house functions as a frontier stockade erected against the disorienting ambiguities of existence in non-community. Business or profession provides an illusion of connection with people whose only connection with us and with one another is conterminous activity within the same "facility" or "structure." At intervals that have grown less and less frequent with the passage of time, the separately orbiting entities of business and home may, for ceremonial reasons, be momentarily joined, and strangers from the one will be imported into the other, given food and enough to drink to ensure that they will not be able to notice that they have nothing to say to one another. Anesthesia is the only possible means of coping with a situation in which nothing can be communicated among people for whom the terms and materials of communication, the shared histories and common assumptions of purpose and value, have ceased to exist. Yet such a situation is only the microcosmic form of the abstraction projected by the media, the vast unstructured and dehistorified macrocosm composed of large and portentous or trivial and meaningless happenings occurring in some remote elsewhere and enacted upon strangers or stranger-celebrities made recognizable by the regular appearance of their faces on the screen, but who are known to us only because, and only *so long as* they are there.

The physical dislocation of the individual from direct relation to his social and public experience has its correlative in an ideological dislocation that has grown increasingly visible over the last ten or fifteen years. There has been a deepening and ever more obsessive preoccupation during this period with the nature and problems not so much of the individual life as of society as a whole—or put another way, the individual life transvaluated into a projection of and a vexation laid upon society as a whole. It is from society seen as a corporate entity that people now try to derive what sense they can of communal relationship and identity, and the effort has most often been made through declarations of allegiance to various political, sexual, racial, or ethnic groups, membership in which is based scarcely at all upon concrete experiences and shared backgrounds (as was the case with minority and subculture membership in the past), but rather upon problems that are conceived of in theoretical and statistical terms as being peculiar to a particular group. Thus, even as personal connection is sought through identification with a group, the group becomes a collective abstraction to which relationship cannot be directly achieved and, therefore, in which further abstraction is the inevitable result. If the loss of the older forms of community has projected us into a formless sociological void, our need to replace community with group membership has projected us even further into the void. For it causes us to see ourselves not as ourselves but as increments of such subcultural categories as female, homosexual, Chicano, or Black, with a further erosion of our sense of the integrity and uniqueness of the individual self.

It follows from this that the currently obsessive quest for a preformulated "role" in some collective has replaced to a large degree the personal quest for a purpose in life and, not incidentally, is depriving the novel of one of its most vital traditional themes. For the search, in all its agony and great potential for destructive risk, that once went on within the precincts of the individual's concrete struggle with his environment tends now to be viewed as a problem belonging to a general social category, a problem with which the individual cannot be expected to cope and, therefore, which is to be projected upon an unjust and oppressive society or politicized into an "issue," which the technocratic powers of legislative reform operating somewhere out there in the void will be required to engage.

There inevitably emerges a state of mind having as its base the belief that life in general is not an experience to be lived but a problem to be solved. The having of experience, from which one may or may not eventually derive certain personal answers, becomes a procedure for which methods of analysis and resolution have been scientifically formulated. This has led to a shift in the individual consciousness from a sense of being the subject of experience to a sense of being its object, so that one examines the experience of other objects in order to ease one's own feeling of unreality at being seen as an object, as a laboratory specimen being acted upon rather than living actively. The displacement of instinct by technological method, with all that it contributes to a further deepening of the passive, dreamlike quality of personal existence, is one of the more deranging phenomena of contemporary life, and it is perhaps the most morbid expression of our desire to die out of the hazards and mistakes of personal existence and enter the nirvana of risk-free problem manipulation where all difficulties are resolvable in a state of serenity which only death can approximate.

It may be paradoxical that this displacement appears to have increased rather than lightened the burden of narcissism that has so heavied the atmosphere of the present time. The individual has not been freed by the view that life is a problem to be solved by the right application of technological method. Rather, he has been forced to become obsessed with the technology of all his personal processes, to see them, as he sees himself and other people, as objects to be analyzed and evaluated for their correctness according to various behavioral measurements and sociological surveys. Since instinct or simply intelligence can no longer be trusted as a guide to feeling and conduct, since the precedent of the past is considered an inhibition from which we are struggling to escape, only technique is left, and it is of course in the area of sexual technique that our narcissistic pre-occupations have become concentrated.

Our attitude toward sex is necessarily ambivalent in this age when the old taboos that once restricted opportunity and performance have been replaced by freedoms that not only widen opportunity but seem almost militantly to demand perfection in the quality and frequency of performance. Through the application of proven technology we have at last achieved the mechanization of ecstasy, and through the scientifically programmed orgasm we have converted into a machine the one function of our bodies that until now has offered us salvation from the machine. Yet, happily, the process is still not quite complete, and the ambivalence in our attitude remains. On the one hand, sex for us is the last of the ultimately personal experiences to carry with it an ever-renewing freshness of sensation in a nerve-deadening world. It is also what we have left of a possibility for transcendence, the discovery of new adventure, the conquest of a continuously reconquerable frontier. As we have grown increasingly abstracted from relationship with our instinctual selves and with others, sex has become the one dependable mode by which the instinctual circuits can be reconnected that join us intimately with people but that once were at least partly extra-sexual in origin. It is undoubtedly true that sex obsesses us today to the extent that opportunities for extra-sexual levels of relationship have died out, to the extent that, locked as we are inside our narcissism, we are forced to make up through our sexuality for the depletion of other socially interactive resources. The result, however, is not a humanization of our sexual impulse, but rather its further mechanization. For the importance we necessarily must give to it is so great that we cannot take the risk of human fallibility, but must seek in technology methods guaranteed to intensify our sexual pleasure to the point where it will compensate us for the loss of so many other pleasures. Thus, we seek in sex as close an approach to divine rapture as science can afford us, sex having become our substitute for religion as scientized sex has replaced nearly every form of human experience including the sexual.

There can be little surprise in the idea that the same forces that have caused us to reduce sex to a problem of methodological strategy have also helped to create our obsession with violence in all the conceivable degrees of its gory magnificence. If so many of the former avenues into emotional intensity are now blocked for us and we have placed upon sex the burden of functioning as the principal source of intensity still available, then we are requiring sex to become an ultimate form of violence. The apocalyptic orgasm we seek in the hope that it will reconnect us with the cosmic circuits of feeling is the sexual equivalent of the apocalyptic thrill we seek through witnessing murder, rape, carnage, and the atomic devastation of cities. Both orgasm and violence are symbols of the psychic journey we hunger to make back to the primal reality where the plastic seals of our narcissism will at last be broken and the tyrannies of repression, the conniving will, and the correct technique overthrown by rapturous frenzies of unlimited fucks and monumental ecstasies of unpunishable murders. Both are of course states of fantasy fulfillment, the kind attainable only in the imagination, and both are voyeuristic in the sense that the satisfaction we find in violence comes from watching it, while our relation to the dream of supernal sexual enjoyment is determined by our preoccupation with watching our own sexual responses and in studying those of other people.

The final result of this interest is pornography, in which violence and other people's sexuality cohabit in precisely the state familiar to most of us as the prevailing condition of contemporary life—unfeeling detachment among human beings who are envisioned as things and to whom we cannot and need not relate except to use them as objects for the discharge of our narcissistic aggressions. But to make the pornographic interest acceptable to the general public it must first be sanctified by marriage to the pieties of science and romantic love and redirected away from self-indulgence toward the universally venerated goal of self-improvement. This has been admirably accomplished by the sexual how-to-do-it publishing industry, which puts sex back where we can most comfortably confront it —under the rubric of popular uplift mechanics as patented and perfected by Jesus Christ, Benjamin Franklin, Dale Carnegie, and Norman Vincent Peale.

On a somewhat less, but not very much less mechanical level, there are the large numbers of best-selling, quasi-fictive confessional novels that have made a more direct appeal to the public imagination because they have to do with characters with whom one may be able to identify and not with clinical tables of erotogenic techniques and statistics. These novels have instructed us over the past several years in the mysteries of other people's sexuality, a knowledge of which we hope will help illuminate our own, and we have been enlightened about, among other things, what it is like to be a male heterosexual, a male homosexual, a male rapist, a male masturbator, and a middle-aged male lover of little girls. But we are still in the first wave of hearing from women about the secrets of female sexuality, that very last frontier within the very last frontier of human erotic exploration. Our current high fascination with the literature on this subject is the result not simply of the voyeurism of men who were brought up assuming that women had no independent sexual appetites and are titillated to learn otherwise, but of the very strong interest among women themselves in discovering, through the experience of other women, something more than they were brought up to know about the nature and meaning of their own appetites.

But the rapid rise to prominence of the novel cast in the form of the female sexual picaresque has the further significance that the journey of the *picara* from childhood innocence through defloration, to orgasm or failure of orgasm, to marriage and happiness or frustration and divorce is so structured that it raises vital questions that may represent the last assaults on illusion and idealism possible in this demythologizing time. For the preoccupation of the anti-heroine of this kind of novel is with self-definition against the adversary force of a society that has too closely confined her within roles created by other people's efforts to do her self-defining for her. Thus, her search is finally not for the apocalyptic orgasm, but for an understanding of whether or not she needs it and wants it, whether she needs a man to help her attain it, whether she needs marriage, household, and motherhood—all the standard and crucial questions to which we have looked to sexuality alone for an answer, only to find that the arena of discourse lies beyond sexuality and encompasses the whole dilemma of human personality and individuality, whether male or female.

For most men in our culture, at least up to this moment, the problem of self-definition may or may not have been directly and consciously engaged. But for those who have sought to create a function and a being against the grain of the official view of what the masculine role should be, the struggle has been, as a rule, an intensely private one. And since the possibilities open to men have always been more numerous, and deviations from the norm subtler, less heretical, and less generally threatening, the struggle has usually been carried forward with no more than a bearable amount of anxiety. But women face the difficulty that the issue of individual autonomy has in our time been propagandized into a collective social concern and militant activist cause. It thus becomes not only a personal problem, but one bound round and round by skeins of public moral imperatives, tissues of self-righteous shoulds and oughts by which women as a corporate minority group have made programmatic the nature and expectations of liberated female existence.

To become separated from socially prescribed modes of being either through atrophy of connection with them or through active rebellion against them is one thing and an oftentimes very traumatic one thing. But to become thus separated and to carry in addition the weight of imperatives imposed from the outside by one's peers is to risk becoming paralyzed in a state of chronic obsessiveness with one's efforts at self-definition, to be lost in the void of narcissism in which the questions repeat over and over again on the turntable of conscience until they annihilate all possibility of an answer: Am I freeing myself or becoming imprisoned in my search for freedom? Am I freeing myself in ways deemed to be correct according to the feminist minority ethos? What am I freeing myself for and from? Am I freeing myself from all those things that in the past limited my freedom, but gave me limits in which to define my function, only to find myself without a means of defining a function in a freedom at least theoretically without limits?

The female writers who have lately been concerned with the plight of their sex and sexuality—and they range over the spectrum of talent from Erica Jong and Gael Greene to Francine du Plessix Gray—have each been obliged in one way or another to confront this eventuality, and it is not surprising that the picaresque journey their books depict so often ends in the discovery that the state of freedom has become as oppressive a tyranny as the tyrannies left behind. Once again we confront the case of the woman abstracted from the received roles of the past coming to that familiar dead-end in which she is also abstracted from herself. Having accepted the corporate conceptions as to which actions represent self-liberation—the choice of career over marriage or single blessedness over double damnation —she becomes aware (or we, in reading her story, become aware) that she is trying to *will* her life to move in certain supposedly liberating directions, while her emotions remain refractory and unsatisfied. Thus, finally, her struggle for freedom is balked not only by the fact that the struggle has become itself a bondage but by the more formidable fact that in trying to find herself she can find nothing to which she is willing to give herself and in the giving achieve the meaning of her freedom.

The self-victimized Stephanie of Francine du Plessix Gray's quite finely written novel, *Lovers and Tyrants,* is in some ways an instructive case in point. Gray is far too sophisticated a writer to allow her heroine to become merely one more megalomaniacal martyr shrieking out of the dank pit of selfness about the injustices attendant upon Being a Woman. Stephanie, in fact, is even equipped with one or two flaws of character that help her to engage our sympathies and that nearly succeed in qualifying her for membership in humanity. Yet she does illustrate what can happen when the effort to live in the service of an abstract idea of oneself as a social problem effectively neutralizes the power to act in the service of what humanity one has.

In this respect she also illustrates that development in contemporary American society whereby we have been largely freed of struggle with material adversity, of having to make our compromises with an unjust and imperfect world, only to arrive at a point where no injustice or imperfection can be tolerated. All life must now be brought before the Supreme Court, there to be tried on the issue of whether or not it is acceptable or relevant to one's idea of personal destiny, freedom, and the realization of one's full creative potential. The Chief Justice here is of course the imperiously imperial self, the sole reality and arbiter in the void of cultural dissociation, and this self must continuously insist upon what is rightfully due it from life, even as it steadfastly refuses to submit to life—presumably out of fear that in so doing its moral rectitude might be sullied or it might perhaps become so caught up in living that it will risk losing all grasp upon what life is supposed to *mean.*

The form best suited to the dramatic development of this dilemma is reverse Pirandello: the author or authorial surrogate in search of his or her true character out of the far more than six characters potentially able to provide liberation into ultimate freedom and creativity. On the most tawdry level the problem finds expression in the spectacle of adults of middle age and presumed intelligence assiduously taking courses in themselves, in learning how to live, in achieving "optimal self-actualization," in "Being a Separate Person," in "Self-Understanding II," in how to win "The Struggle To Be Me"—these last being actual or approximate titles of courses offered at certain quite reputable adult education establishments.

However, it need scarcely to be said that Gray's Stephanie is anything but tawdry. She is highly sophisticated, civilized, very bright, and attractive, and she is only genteelly aware of the narcissistic force of her motivation. For her the burden of guilt is squarely on the shoulders of life, whose manifold frustrations and tyrannies consistently subvert her best efforts to discover and liberate the real Stephanie. Curiously enough, the chief obstacle life imposes between her and her unspecified destiny is love, which in her view is always an invasion of selfness and a persecuting force, since it demands a reciprocation she cannot bring herself to make. In the course of her development Stephanie becomes involved with a series of lover-tyrants, all of whom are left to languish in various degrees of unrequitedness. First, there is the wretched, parasitical governess of her childhood years in Paris, a woman who smothers her in so much sticky emotion and who demands—but of course does not get—so much in return that she becomes a primary figure of guilt haunting Stephanie well into her adult life. Then there are the many men with whom she has affairs, each of them unworthy of her, exploitative of her, and threatening to her freedom because they also try to impose upon her the unreasonable requirement that she have some feeling for them. Her marriage to Paul, the silent, conservative, house-proud architect, promises to relieve her of having to meet this requirement. Paul is obtuse enough to love her without seeming to be conscious of whether or not she loves him back. But his very obtuseness, his totally uncritical acceptance of himself and her, proves to be the worst tyranny of all because it represents a denial of her reality as a person.

Finally (and whether this occurs in actuality or fantasy, Gray does not make clear), Stephanie, now middle-aged, takes up with a thoroughly repulsive young man who uses her quite openly as a substitute mother and a provider of luxuries. At the end of the novel Stephanie seems on the verge of getting rid of him and announces her decision to "live alone, or with others, for myself." "I've done it again, kiddo," she says. "I've done it better than ever, this time I've exorcised myself of one hell of a bunch of oppressors. . . . Here, at last, is a beginning."

Thus, she throws off the chains of her victimization by others and is free at last to become—what? Surely, Gray cannot really mean what she seems to be saying in answer to this or perhaps she is unaware of what she seems to be saying. For beneath the surface of Stephanie's story and challenging the authority of her point of view, the materials of another, perhaps unintended but extremely interesting interpretation become visible. It would now appear that Stephanie has all along, at the behest of whatever unconscious motives, quite carefully selected people who will love her and give her the emotional security she needs without deserving to be loved by her in return. Thus, in a position of freedom within dependency she is able to devote her full energies to keeping alive the idea she has of herself as a woman who *could* fulfill herself if only she could get rid of these people and their tyrannical possessiveness.

However, the evidence is clear that she needs them not only to give her security but to afford her an excuse for *not* fulfilling herself—fulfillment, when it does not involve specific ambition or the exercise of a particular talent, being in her case only a self-flattering abstraction providing her with the illusion that she is a person who, if she were not tyrannized, would be capable of some important achievement. At the end she appears to have gained an understanding of her situation and evidently does free herself of her "oppressors." But this does not lead her to discover her purpose in life in the sense of identifying a career or a possible outlet for her creativity. Rather, she has discovered that she no longer needs the oppression of others to prevent her from achieving what she now quite accurately perceives to be her true purpose in life. She can now enter happily into a love affair with the one person who is worthy of her love and whose love she can return without having the feeling that she is being tyrannized. The idea of freedom and fulfillment has given way to the emotional fact of narcissistic entrapment. Stephanie is free to love herself in the manner to which she has always been accustomed, but with the difference that she will do so henceforward quite openly and guiltlessly.

It is unlikely that Gray intended the conclusion of the novel to be read in this way, for there is no edge of irony in her treatment of it. But if there is validity in such a reading, as I believe there is, then the implications would seem to enforce some of the observations I made earlier: that individual fulfillment in much of the new fiction concerning women is more an unspecified idea than the product of a clearly perceived program of action, and that there often remains a considerable separation between a woman's determination to find fulfillment and her need to give herself emotionally—or even to seek involvements that will *obstruct* her efforts to find fulfillment. In Stephanie's case of course the solution is love of self, a radical solution, but given her character and the evidence of her narrative, perhaps the only logical one. When all relationships prove to be inadequate or stifling, when there is a strong urge for freedom without the support of a concrete purpose, all that remains is the imperial self cultivating its admirable virtues for its own limitless delectation.

CHAPTER II

The Voice in the Void

It is conventional to notice that the growth of the novel form has been accompanied in modern times by a steadily increasing emphasis upon individual consciousness, the inward-turning, ever more solipsistic preoccupations of the imperial self. We now accept this as a truism, which, unlike many, has its truth, just as we also accept the idea that the increased attention to consciousness has led to the novel's own greatly enlarged sense of itself as an art form and to its recently renewed tendency toward self-parodistic effects, which so often foreshadow the appearance of some new mutation within the form.

But what has been less frequently noticed is the particular relation established in the classic modern novel between individual consciousness and the physical or social environment in which it is set down. If *Ulysses* is prototypical of the modern novel of consciousness, it must be remembered that Joyce's emphasis—except in the passages devoted to Stephen Dedalus—is less upon the consciousness initially conscious of itself than upon consciousness as a medium—albeit an oftentimes prismatic medium—through which the appearances of the external world are communicated to us. There may be considerable subjectivity in the selection and the perception of the elements to be communicated, depending on the subtlety and complexity of the perceiving mind in any given case. But we are essentially viewing through the ratiogenative processes of that mind an environment which we are fairly dependably certain is *there*—except of course when we know, as we do in the "Nighttown" scenes, that the perceiving mind is in fact hallucinating.

If we further consider novels that are not usually seen as novels of consciousness—let us say the novels of Hemingway or Fitzgerald—it is apparent that the perceptional processes of the characters lack the obsessive, self-observing quality one associates with the narcissistic intelligence of a Stephen Dedalus. At the same time they function only in an intermittent and narrow way to put us into possession of the crowded appearances of the environment in which they operate. Rather, they are focused upon and limited by efforts on the part of the characters to achieve and maintain positions of strength or understanding as they confront situations in their environment that challenge their strength or understanding. Thus, Nick Carraway tries to comprehend the enigma of Gatsby and ultimately to gain a perspective of moral judgment, which will enable him fairly to evaluate Gatsby. To be sure, he does in the process perceive various elements in his environment and personal situation that may have only the remotest relation to the central problem of evaluating Gatsby. But the nature and function of his perceptions are not by themselves in question, not even at those moments when what *is* in question is the accuracy of the information he is being given or how best to interpret the actions of others. These are not matters of which he is conscious or about which he is self-conscious, since the purpose of his perceiving is not to reveal the *manner* of his perceiving, but to illuminate the primary issue of Gatsby. However, all else in the novel is by no means merely window-dressing. Much of it, in fact, works, and works brilliantly, to thicken, darken, and make tragically ironic the primary issue. But it is never seen—as it might have been in a novel by Joyce—as material whose presence is justified mainly by the *quality* of the perceptiveness brought to bear upon it.

The characters of Hemingway come closest to achieving something like what we normally think of as perception only when they are forced to by the exigencies of war, sex, hazardous sport, hunting, and fishing—where the interest lies both in a character's heightened sensitivity to very immediate conditions of personal risk and in the nature of the values, the quality of the psychic resources, which he is able to summon in self-defense against them. In the case of both writers it might be said that consciousness exists as an instrument of action and a gauge of will—although we recognize that for Hemingway, to whom all action is finally a question of the purity of style so disciplined by will that it becomes instinctive, consciousness emerges as the adversary of instinct, hence the enemy of style.

Clearly, the most advanced contemporary fiction has developed along the course laid down by Joyce, for in so much of it one notices that consciousness become acutely obsessive *self-consciousness* functions more and more as the medium as well as the substance of narrative. This would seem to suggest that while our writers have learned from Joyce, the force of history has propelled them beyond Joyce into a radical dissociation from the kind of environment so minutely perceived in *Ulysses*. As through the passage of time the connections have diminished that once forced us to be aware of and actively to engage the challenges of a specific social or physical world—whether a city such as Dublin, the society of the very rich, or a bullring in Spain—awareness has come increasingly to be awareness of the *process* of awareness, and private fantasies, fears, and paranoias have replaced the real adventures and menaces that once accompanied the effort to survive within an engageable environment. Just as a prisoner in prolonged solitary confinement must be able to sleep and dream or he will surely go mad, so the person confined in solitary self-awareness must dream up, out of the waste matter of his subconscious, an environment which he can assume he inhabits, even if in some important part of himself he knows that he is creating it as he goes along. The distance between fantasy and fact, illusion and reality, fear and any discoverable cause for fear is finally eliminated, since the only validating measure of perception is what one *thinks* to be true, just as the only perceptible measure of experience is the act of thinking, the externalization of or projection upon the external world of the compulsive perceptional patterns of one's neurosis —until at last the projection becomes, for all practical purposes, the external world.

In the novel the originating form of this process is undoubtedly the French *récit,* in which the soloist is himself his own solo, the form in its several variations of Sartre's *Nausea*, Camus's *The Stranger*, and some of the fiction of Gide, Beckett, and Céline. Among contemporary American novelists there is—to take one representative case—John Hawkes who has produced several very pure examples of a fiction in which the supposedly objective milieu is composed of both actual people and things and what the observer perceives, through the aberrations of his personal vision, to be actual. As the standards for measuring reality become more relative, hence more personal, there finally proves to be, in Hawkes's world, no effective way of distinguishing objective from subjective, nor for that matter is there particular purpose in trying to do so, since what the observer *perceives* to be true is precisely the meaning of his sensibility.

It would also seem—if one can judge by the novels of Hawkes and several of his contemporaries—that the breakdown of connection between the self and an engageable social milieu, the fading into each other of subjective perception and objective reality, must induce in the perceiver extreme feelings of anxiety and paranoia. For if a social milieu cannot be personally engaged and in the process familiarized into trustworthiness, then it becomes an enemy whose behavior is wholly unpredictable, and one can never be sure whether, in its role as an inscrutable other, it will behave according to benevolent or malevolent motives. By the same token, if inner and outer realities become interchangeable, then reality can be whatever one thinks it is—or it can become whatever blind chance or random impulse may cause it to become. "A man was shot in the park today," says Joseph Heller in *Something Happened*. "Nobody knows why." "No one's in charge." The separation of action from any knowable cause is not merely inexplicable. It invites the observer to synthesize from the inexplicableness a vision of a reality that is operating quite independently of his understanding and participation, and that therefore causes him to attribute to it the darkest motives his conspiratorial imagination can conceive.

It follows from this that the form in which such a vision is now most commonly dramatized is vociferous *external* monologue— the Joycean technique turned inside out and expressing no longer alienation *from* but alienation *in the company of* others

—just as for the same reasons the habit of uninterruptible monology is the most pervasive and irritating social mannerism of our time. In a culture in which only the self seems, however tenuously, to be real and only one's own thoughts have validity, there can be little chance for conversation, since that implies both a belief in the reality of other people and a desire to share their views. But if these basic necessities of communication are missing, there can only be voices raised to drown out other voices, only statements that are almost always assertions and almost never replies—assorted imperial selves jabbering out of the vacuum of their unbreachable insularity.

Monologue, in short, is the natural solipsistic form, just as paranoia is the inevitable solipsistic condition. Hence, given the high incidence of that condition at this time, it is logical that we should have a very large number of novels in which the narrative medium is a raging voice and the subliminal message is how infinitely more definable is the quality of that rage than are any of its possible causes. Saul Bellow, Philip Roth, Walker Percy, and Joseph Heller among others have all written fervidly monologistic novels. But the case of Roth is of particular interest because in a sense his whole career up to now has represented a sustained effort to deal creatively with some of the circumstances in contemporary life that have helped to produce the current obsessiveness with the monologistic form.

In 1961, Roth published a remarkable essay entitled "Writing American Fiction" which attracted considerable attention at the time and has since come to be regarded as something of a classic critical statement. The essay was written with all the self-assurance and high moral severity one could expect to find in a young writer who had been rather extravagantly overpraised for his first book and who might be forgiven for considering himself qualified to sit in judgment upon his elders and contemporaries. What impresses one most in rereading it today is the accuracy with which Roth was able to diagnose the more serious problems facing the writer of fiction in a society clearly gone berserk, and to forecast developments such as Black Humor, the New Journalism, and fictionalized autobiography, which in 1961 were barely emergent as major literary trends. But the essay has also taken on over the years a certain poignant dimension. For in predicting the future course of American fiction in the sixties and seventies and castigating some of his fellow writers for the creative adjustments they had made, or failed to make, to the dilemma he described, Roth unwittingly prophesied the course of his own future career as a novelist. Most of the errors and evasions of artistic responsibility he detected in the work of others were to be precisely those to which he himself was later to succumb.

The most widely quoted observation in the essay has to do with the writer's feelings of bafflement and frustration when confronted with the grotesque improbability of most of the events of contemporary life. ". . . the American writer in the middle of the 20th Century has his hands full in trying to understand, and then describe, and then make *credible* much of the American reality. It stupifies, it sickens, it infuriates, and finally it is even a kind of embarrassment to one's own meager imagination. The actuality is continually outdoing our talents . . ." Roth then proceeded to discuss the work of certain of his contemporaries and to find in much of it evidence of a failure to engage the American reality—an inevitable failure, he believed, because "what will be [the writer's] subject? His landscape? It is the tug of reality, its mystery and magnetism, that leads one into the writing of fiction—what then when one is not mystified but stupified? not drawn but repelled? It would seem that what we might get would be a high proportion of historical novels or contemporary satire—or perhaps just nothing. No books."

Roth cited Mailer's *Advertisements for Myself* as the expression of "a despair so great that the man who bears it, or is borne by it, seems for the time being . . . to have given up on making an imaginative assault upon the American experience, and has become instead the champion of a kind of public revenge"— exactly the kind, one might propose, that Roth himself has been taking upon the public through various of his later novels as his own power to assault the American experience has steadily declined.

Later in the essay he criticized Salinger for creating characters whose sole response to the contemporary world is to have nervous breakdowns or commit suicide or retreat into a specious mysticism, while Malamud's characters seemed to him to be people who exist outside the realities of the current historical situation and who function as metaphors for general human possibilities rather than as representations of existing social types. Roth next accused Bellow and Styron of imaginative falsification, most notably in *Henderson the Rain King* and *Set This House on Fire* where the action is resolved in gestures or statements of unearned optimism and philosophical affirmation. Herbert Gold particularly troubled Roth because Gold, in his view, was the perfect example of the writer so completely turned away from the contemporary scene that he is left with nothing but his narcissism. In Gold's work "there is a good deal of delight in the work of his own hand. And, I think, with the hand itself" —a statement that, coming from a man who was later to write *Portnoy's Complaint*, the most hand-infatuated novel in American literary history, is surely rich in ironic portent.

Roth again might have been displaying prescience about his own future creative incarnations, this time as the author of *My Life as a Man*, in his final comments on Gold. His "extravagant prose, his confessional tone (the article about divorce; then the several prefaces and appendices about his own divorce—my ex-wife says this about me, etc.; then finally the story about divorce)—all of this seems to have meaning to me in terms of this separation . . . the not-so-friendly relationship between the writer and the culture. . . . I must say I am not trying to sell selflessness. . . . The writer pushes before our eyes . . . personality, in all its separateness and specialness. Of course the mystery of personality is nothing less than the writer's ultimate concern . . . at its worst, however, as a form of literary onanism, it seriously curtails the fictional possibilities, and may perhaps be thought of, and sympathetically so, as a symptom of the writer's loss of the community as subject . . . it may be that when the (cultural) predicament produces in the writer not only feelings of disgust, rage, and melancholy but impotence too, he is apt to lost heart and finally . . . turn to other matters or to other worlds; or to the self, which may, in a variety of ways, become his subject or even the impulse for his technique. What I have tried to point out is that the sheer fact of self, the vision of self as inviolable, powerful, and nervy, self as the only real thing in an unreal environment, that that vision has given to some writers joy, solace, and muscle." Roth's own decision to seek his subject through the exploration of self, in particular within the narcissistic imperatives of the self at war with the derangements of contemporary life, was to be made some years after these sentences were written, and it proved to be the crucial and determining act of his later career.

Given his premises as stated in the essay and his perhaps excessive sensitivity to the social conditions in which the creative imagination is obliged to function, there was undoubtedly no other decision he could have made. For ten years following the appearance of *Goodbye, Columbus* in 1959, Roth struggled to find a form that would contain and objectify his sternly adversary vision of American culture, and in his two massive novels of the early and middle sixties, *Letting Go* and *When She Was Good*, he experimented with greater effectiveness than is generally recognized with the traditional form of the realistic social novel. But the difficulty of this form for Roth was that it demanded a sense of thematic coherence he did not possess, as well as a social experience definable in terms of certain implicit concepts of communal order which, as he well knew, contemporary society did not possess. As a result, Roth found himself caught in a predicament that, to one degree or another, has confounded American writers ever since Melville: he had vast quantities of material, but he could not discover or possess a subject. All he could do was describe and document at infinite length the experiences of his characters, record every word of their interminable and mostly trivial conversations, and in that way produce a certain effect of life—busy, abrasive, vibrant, but finally one-dimensional and incoherent. It also became apparent in these novels that Roth suffered from two primary weaknesses that severely limited his ability to work successfully with objectively created characters in a realistically presented social milieu: he had no power to identify or sympathize with characters who were not to some degree extensions or idealizations of himself, and his natural tendency was to recoil in horror from contemporary experience and to treat it with the contempt of one who feels that he alone is worthy of salvation.

In short, on the evidence of these novels it was clear that the form most congenial to Roth was the novel of narcissism, just as his strongest gift was for the tragicomedy of paranoia, and it happened that in *Portnoy's Complaint* he was able to coordinate form and gift to extraordinary effect. Yet there was still a lingering urge in Roth to make the kind of direct assault on the social and political realities of our time which in his essay he had criticized some of his contemporaries for failing to make, and he continued to search for a form that would give focus to the assault. He accordingly produced after *Portnoy's Complaint* three very different and very bad novels: *Our Gang*, a heavy-handed and adolescent satire of the Nixon administration which only verified the truth of Roth's observation that "the actuality is continually outdoing our talents," particularly when the actuality is Richard Nixon; *The Breast*, a baffling and pretentious scrap of psychological fantasy that is ghoulish in its tastelessness; and *The Great American Novel*, an even more baffling mélange of hyperkinetic writing about the mythology of baseball. Clearly, it was impossible for Roth to deal successfully in fiction with either the public realities or the various fantasy worlds of contemporary life, and the reasons were precisely those he had recognized in 1961. The experience of our time was stupifying and infuriating to the writer not merely because it was so often more incredible than anything he could imagine, but because it seemed to have no relation to the individual self. That, in fact, was the prime feature of its incredibility.

For a writer of Roth's particular talent and temperament there is only one reliable measure of credibility—what the self feels and thinks—and only one compelling interest—what the self experiences—in Roth's case, how events and people, especially women, have assaulted his sanity, thwarted or provoked his sexuality, and outraged his sense of moral virtue. This is the story he told in *Portnoy's Complaint*, and he told it again in rather different terms in *My Life as a Man*, his eighth work of fiction, published in 1974. But the fact which in the former was partially obscured by the absorbing joys of book-length masturbation is in the latter revealed in full clarity: although Roth is a fine stylist and may be the funniest serious writer in America, he is gravely deficient in a sense of the novel form; he has no firm understanding of what his novels are supposed to mean; and he has no subject matter except fanatical self-infatuation.

His strategy in *My Life as a Man* is to try to convert these weaknesses into literary capital by making them part of the contrived architectural and thematic design of the novel. The theory behind this presumably is that an author is permitted to do anything in a novel provided he can convince the reader that he did it deliberately, in the service of some however obscure artistic intention. Roth divides his narrative into two sections, the first purporting to be a fictional account written by a young novelist named Peter Tarnopol of the adventures of a young novelist named Nathan Zuckerman, the second presenting Tarnopol's ostensibly autobiographical account of the actual experiences of his from which some of the events of the first section have been distilled. Throughout this monologue Tarnopol speculates continually about the relationship between his own life and that of his fictional alter ego, expresses bafflement at the complexity of the problem, and seems to be trying to create the impression that his (and Roth's) novel is really about the effort of the novelist to define and explore the connection between life and art. The writing of *My Life as a Man* would thus become for Roth-Tarnopol not only a search for but a *record of* the search for the novel's meaning; the life-art relationship is given dramatic objectification in the novel's two-part structure; and the expectation is that the novel's theme is to be discovered in Tarnopol's struggle to make fictional use of the materials of his life.

This technique of incorporating the author's creative difficulties into the work that is generating the difficulties is of course an old and familiar one, and so is the technique of bringing the author or his surrogate into the work and depicting him in the act of writing what one is in the act of reading. Gide, Huxley, Nabokov, and others have made brilliant use of many variations of such devices and have created with them an effect of conflicting illusion and reality that has formed one of the most common thematic perspectives of literary modernism. But in Roth's hands they become merely tricks employed to produce a mirage of complication evidently intended to conceal a feebleness of conception. There is actually no earned relationship between the fictional experiences of Zuckerman and the "real life" experiences of Tarnopol; hence, there is no thematic justification for the presence of both men in the novel. Tarnopol might as well have devoted the entire novel to the story of his own life or Roth might have devoted it to the story of his. Whatever advantage he gained through the use of Tarnopol and Zuckerman may have been of some value in a defense against a charge of libel, but literarily it appears meaningless.

In addition to the complications of structure and the refracting perspectives of his fictional personae, Roth resorts to other devices in his effort to give the appearance of artistic deliberation to effects he seems to have sensed might be viewed as artistic flaws. At one point in Tarnopol's narrative, for example, Roth introduces, and by introducing apparently hopes to forestall, an obvious criticism of his novel. Tarnopol has sent his brother Morris copies of the two stories which comprise the Zuckerman narrative, and Morris responds in part as follows:

> What is it with you Jewish writers? Madeleine Herzog, Deborah Rojack, the cutie-pie castrator in *After the Fall*, and isn't the desirable shiksa of *A New Life* a kvetch and titless in the bargain? And now, for the further delight of the rabbis and the reading public, Lydia Zuckerman, that Gentile tomato. Chicken soup in every pot, and a Grushenka in every garage. With all the Dark Ladies to choose from, you luftmenschen can really pick 'em. Peppy, why are you still wasting your talent on that Dead End Kid? Leave her to Heaven, okay? . . . Peppy, *enough with her already!*

Throughout the novel Tarnopol is repeatedly accused of fanatical preoccupation with his guilts, his Jewishness, his marriage, and his ego. His psychiatrist, Dr. Spielvogel, who is cutely resurrected from *Portnoy's Complaint*, considers him to be "among the nation's top young narcissists in the arts" and diagnoses his troubles as stemming from "narcissistic self-dramatization." He also writes him a letter of criticism of the Zuckerman stories. In fact, almost all the people in Tarnopol's life—his relatives, mistresses, students, wife—write him letters about the stories, and they call attention to shortcomings that Roth has had ample opportunity to discover his own writing possesses. But it is, after all, *Tarnopol's* writing that is being criticized, and because it is, Roth nearly succeeds in having it both ways. He can disarm critics by pointing out his own artistic flaws before they do, and he can assign them to the work of a fictional writer who is not himself but to whom, as his creator, he is superior. The trouble is that there is actually no discernible difference between Tarnopol and Roth, just as there is no discernible reason except perhaps a legalistic one why Tarnopol rather than Roth should be acting as narrator. Tarnopol is never evaluated by Roth even though he is criticized by just about everybody else, and Roth never achieves sufficient dramatic distance from him to make it clear what he thinks and, therefore, what the reader is supposed to think about Tarnopol's character and behavior. There is, furthermore, no evidence that Tarnopol is intended to function as an untrustworthy narrator, the kind who is characterized by his errors of perception and extravagant responses. His is the only point of view in his story, and those moments when another might become authoritative and contradictory of his are never exploited—presumably because he and his creator are at all times in complete agreement.

My Life as a Man is, in short, a totally solipsistic novel, which may very well make it a perfect expression of the times. It is created out of the materials of exactly the kind of estrangment from the public culture Roth described in his essay. Its form is the endless ranting monologue; its content is guilt, anxiety, and acute paranoia; its appropriate setting is the psychiatrist's office where, as was literally the case in *Portnoy's Complaint*, the only sound is the sound of the narrator's voice. Nothing in the world is real except that voice, all our separate, complaining voices.

But Roth's problem is that he cannot function as his own psychiatrist. He cannot find the meaning of his anguish or his anger; hence, we cannot. All he can do is talk, talk, talk, sometimes brilliantly, sometimes tediously, but always toward a point that is never reached because it does not exist. What he is really up to is—to use his own phrase—a form of literary onanism.

The voice of Bob Slocum, the narrator-protagonist of Joseph Heller's *Something Happened*, is less autoerotic than autistic, a medium for the projection of fantasies that are more apocalyptic than sexual and of realities that one can only assume are more fanciful than actual. As is the case with Roth's compulsive monologists, the precise extent of Slocum's over-reaction to his predicament is extremely hard to determine. One *assumes* that he is deluded a large part of the time, but one cannot know precisely to what degree because his descriptions of himself, his experiences, and his responses to them constitute the primary evidence from which a measurement might be made. It is only by comparing what he believes to be true with what would seem to be a rational or balanced assessment of the facts he gives us that the extent of his untrustworthiness can be approximately understood. But one is placed so exactly within the angle of Slocum's vision and is held there so scrupulously that distinctions between fantasy and fact, paranoia and justifiable wariness, can be arrived at only with the greatest difficulty. All that is *given* in the novel is the material of his consciousness verbalized, however imperfectly or hysterically, by his narrative. One is allowed to view only obliquely the experience to which his consciousness reacts and out of which the extravagant preoccupations of his narrative are formed. There is, in fact, only a minimal amount of objectively rendered experience to be found anywhere in the novel. What occurs is, for the most part, what Slocum thinks or imagines occurs. His voice is the messenger of the narrative and at the same time the creator of its message.

Yet it would appear that this is just the point Heller wishes to make about the character of Slocum's situation and the environment he ostensibly inhabits. His perceptions represent the most authoritative measure of his situation because he exists as a mind encapsulated in a bubble of self-awareness afloat in a void left by the disappearance of all other modes of authoritative measure. The most poignant feature of his personal and public life is how little it has to do with anything remotely recognizable as a personal and public life. His environment, in fact, has been quite deliberately engineered by the various bureaucratic agencies of the current mass dystopianism so that it will contain no conflict or contingency, so that it cannot be engaged, affirmed, or denied by anyone within it. This is its achieved character and, by the standards of the prevailing corporate metaphysics, its supreme virtue. It has been created in conformity to the dogma most reverenced in the modern technocratic era: that the freedom to take the risks of one's life in an adversary environment has been abolished in favor of a programmed function within an affluent security that has been happily sanitized of both freedom and risk—the system guaranteeing in return for the dutiful performance of one's function that nothing will happen to anyone ever again. If at any time there should be problems, one can be certain they will prove to be solvable before they have a chance to become problematical.

Here is Slocum's description:

> The company is benevolent. The people, for the most part, are nice, and the atmosphere, for the most part, is convivial. The decor of the offices . . . is bright and colorful. There is lots of orange and lots of sea green. There are lots of office parties. We get all legal holidays off and take days off with pay whenever we need them. We have many three- and four-day weekends. . . . Every two weeks we are paid with machine-processed checks manufactured of stiff paper . . . that are patterned precisely with neat, rectangular holes and words of formal, official warning . . . that the checks must not be spindled, torn, defaced, stapled, or mutilated in any other way. (They must only be cashed.) If not for these words, it would never occur to me to do anything else with my check but deposit it. What would happen . . . if I did spindle, fold, tear, deface, staple, and mutilate it? What would happen if . . . I disobeyed?
>
> I know what would happen. Nothing would happen. And the knowledge depresses me. . . . I suppose it is just about impossible for someone like me to rebel anymore. . . . I have lost the power to upset things that I had as a child; I can no longer change my environment or even disturb it seriously.

They would simply fire and forget me as soon as I tried. They would file me away. That's what will happen to Martha the typist when she finally goes crazy. She'll be fired and forgotten. She'll be filed away. She'll be given sick pay, vacation pay, and severance pay. She'll be given money from the pension fund and money from the profit-sharing fund, and then all traces of her will be hidden safely out of sight inside some old green cabinet for dead records in another room on another floor or in a dusty warehouse somewhere that nobody visits more than once or twice a year and few people in the company even know exists. . . .

This sinisterly tranquilizing situation gives Slocum no comfort whatever. Its benignant inhumanity provokes and at the same time blandly absorbs his anxiety, even as it offers no tangible justification for it. He has been programmed—he thinks in childhood or at some time back before a mysterious something happened to him and to life—to deal aggressively with his environment, while his environment has been programmed not to deal with him at all, except insofar as he can be manipulated as a thing. If he resists, it will simply file him away into instant oblivion. He is driven, therefore, to populate his fantasy world with enemies who will serve as objects for the hostility he feels but cannot externalize in any other way.

In the office in which I work there are five people of whom I'm afraid. Each of these five people is afraid of four people (excluding overlaps), for a total of twenty, and each of these twenty people is afraid of six people, making a total of one hundred and twenty people who are feared by at least one person. . . .

Slocum believes this to be true and needs, for the sake of what sanity he has, to go on believing it. He requires conditions of mistrust and competition, whether real or imaginary, in order to feel real to himself and to keep alive the illusion that he is real to others. But the problem is that he knows that his efforts to manufacture these conditions are pointless because there is no interchange, in which they can be made to exist. And that of social context, no environment of human feeling or personal course is the reason why his hostility is so excruciating: there is nothing out there to provoke it, hence nothing on which to discharge it.

Even at home where he lives a parody of the life ordained by our society to be comfortable and pleasant, the life deodorized of want and contingency, Slocum is as entombed in isolation as he was in the office. Although the sex he has with his still attractive wife is frequent and good, the pleasure he finds in it is vitiated by the absence of all possibility for a relationship in which they can become real to each other. His wife is a sullen stranger who secretly drinks in the afternoons and is beginning to flirt at parties. His teen-age daughter is both sullen and surly and devotes herself to attacking her parents because she believes they do not love her. Actually, Slocum hates her much of the time not only because she behaves hatefully, but because, as is the case in his world generally, the terms are missing by which he might have defined and engaged her humanity. In place of these terms there have grown up confections of abstracting sociological clichés that reduce persons to statistics and that are insidious just because they convert the vital uniqueness of personal experience into the dead predictability of technological phenomena. It is not at all surprising that Slocum sees his daughter as a stereotype of the youth-cult collective, for that, we can fairly conclude, is precisely what she is and, given her circumstances in the age, cannot help but be. Accordingly, Slocum is able, with much malice and acuity, to anticipate the course of her future development as if she were a construct of graphable behavior patterns synthesized from the results of a house-to-house survey:

> She will drink whiskey for a while . . . then stop; then start in again after she's been married several years and drink whiskey regularly from then on. . . . She will have two children or three and be divorced . . . and she will marry a second time if she and the children are still young when the first marriage breaks up. . . . She will smoke marijuana . . . if she isn't doing so already. . . . She will get laid. . . . She will go wild for a while (and think she is free), have all-night revels and bull sessions, complain about her teachers and curriculum require-

ments, have no interest in any of her academic subjects and get passing grades in all with very little work. . . . She will experiment with pep pills (ups), barbiturates (downs), mescaline, and LSD, if LSD remains in vogue; she will have group sex (at least once), homosexual sex (at least once, and at least once more with a male present as a spectator and participant), be friendly with fags, poets, snobs, nihilists, and megalomaniacs, dress like other girls, have abortions . . . and sleep, for a while, with Negroes, even though she will probably enjoy none of it, and might really not want to do *any* of it (She is a strong-minded girl who is far too weak to withstand a popular trend.) . . . she will emerge, if she is lucky, from this period of wanton profligacy and determined self-expression . . . feeling tense, worthless, spent, and remorseful, having searched everywhere and found nothing, with no ego at all, and pine for just one good, stable, interesting man to marry . . . and live happily ever after with.

Yet Slocum's solipsistic vision may dominate, but in the nature of things cannot have unchallenged authority in the novel. There are aspects of his experience he describes, but does not or cannot afford to comprehend, and there are others he evaluates inadequately or does not evaluate at all. That in fact finally provides the measure of his solipsism. We see around and behind its circumscriptions and come at last to understand its perversity. His wife and daughter, for example, do not exist completely in his presentation of them, and exactly because the presentation is unsupported by adequate perception. Slocum responds to them in terms of the various ways in which they irritate, challenge, frighten, or demand a response from him. But he is oblivious to the hunger and anguish that prompt their demands. The daughter in particular exists in a state of chronic starvation for his love. The wife is periodically appeased because she mistakes the frequent and good sex she enjoys with him for the tenderness she really craves and he cannot provide. Sex for him is discharge of anger and frustration, a reprieve from emotional frigidity and from a boredom that is as interminable as his description of it. It is only in his fantasies that sex takes on an edge of adventurous feeling and then only when intercourse is promised but never achieved—as was the case with Virginia, the girl who was the first to arouse him and keep him aroused, but whom he was never able to take to bed. Slocum masturbates on the memory of Virginia's lips, breasts, and thighs even when he is having vigorous intercourse with his wife. His fantasies about Virginia have survived for many years because they have remained fantasies and so have escaped the inevitable dissolution into dead routine of his real sexual experience. There is perhaps too heavy an irony in the fact that on the one occasion when circumstances shock Slocum into an expression of genuine feeling, when his fear that something dreadful will happen seems to have been confirmed by his son's accident, he himself is the cause of disaster. Seeing the boy lying on the sidewalk, blood gushing from him, Slocum clasps him tightly in his arms. He is dying, Slocum believes. "He looks beggingly at me for help. His screams are piercing. I can't bear to see him suffering such agony and fright. I have to do something. I hug his face deeper into the crook of my shoulder . . . I squeeze." "Death," says the doctor, "was due to asphyxiation. The boy was smothered."

But it is in accordance with the nullifying logic of Slocum's world that this tragedy should be immediately absorbed into abstraction and disinfected of its horror. The system in its malignant benevolence simply files it away, and Slocum's life resumes as if nothing had happened to disrupt it. He is promoted to a better job which gives him a gratifying authority over others and the privilege of playing golf with "a much better class of people." At the end of the novel Martha the typist suffers a mental breakdown, as Slocum has always known she one day would, and he skillfully directs the arrangements whereby she too is filed away and forgotten. "Everyone," he observes, "seems pleased with the way I've taken command."

Something Happened is an extremely bleak exposition of the process by which experience in our culture has been demythified not by or within literary works, but rather by the forces of historical change and moral dissolution within the culture itself. Slocum's story is one in which the transcendental meanings that were once associated with love, sexuality, marriage, parenthood, and professional success are not *being* stripped away, but have already been stripped away. This is what the novel is about—

human existence unsupported by the conventional sustaining ideas or illusions of value that might give it value, an existence in which the clearest perception is of the omnipresent threat of disaster and of the passing of some former intensity and significance whose nature eternally eludes the memory.

Like so many heroes of contemporary American fiction Slocum sees life in entropic terms. We decline from our beginnings, not grow beyond them. When sensations cease to be new, they do not mellow or become rich. They simply lose meaning. There are no second acts in American lives, not merely because adult values are so precariously held to in this place and time but because the values of youth are never invalidated by age. They are only left behind in the meaningless drift of history in which at an indefinable moment something happened to make them unrecapturable.

CHAPTER III

No One in Charge

Bob Slocum's voice drones in an interminable monologue out of a void in which the only sound is the sound of itself. It ranges obsessively over the past and present, trying to articulate the incomprehensible, seeking always to talk its way out of what is for Heller the ultimate terrifying helplessness—the inability to identify or confront the forces that are destroying one's life and preparing one's death. But the deeply lodged suspicion in *Something Happened*—as in so much contemporary fiction—is that there is no one at all in charge, that Kafka's castle is in fact empty, that there is no crime for which one eternally stands condemned, no order behind organization, no system behind bureaucratic structure, no governing principle behind government, that what is happening is happening for no reason, and that there is absolutely nothing to be done about it because the causes responsible cannot be located and the very idea of responsibility may have lost all meaning.

This is the nihilistic perception behind Heller's third novel, *Good as Gold*. Yet in spite of it he has been able to generate what is at times an almost joyous comedy out of the depths of apocalypse and to identify and engage some of the specific social conditions that have caused the vision of apocalypse to become a defining feature of the present time. Heller has accomplished this through his particularly effective use of two seemingly very different kinds of narrative materials—the Jewish family experience (his first attempt in fiction to draw on this experience) and a wildly phantasmagoric rendition of the Washington political scene. His protagonist, Bruce Gold, is a minor Jewish intellectual,

academic, and essayist who plans to write an "abstract autobiography" based on the history of Jewish life in America, a
book that is never written but that the novel, to a certain
extent, becomes.

Gold moves back and forth between Washington and various
dreadful meetings with his relatives in New York, seeing no
connection between the two except that Washington promises
to be a glamorous escape from the wretchedness of the family.
Yet it is one of the considerable brilliances of the novel that
although they are never explicitly paralleled, the Washington
and the family experiences can finally be seen to have a portentous
similarity. Both in fact represent aspects of the same condition,
the dehumanization and derangement of life that follow on the
collapse of those values that once made humanity and rationality
necessary.

As Heller portrays it, the trashed and decaying environment of
South Brooklyn becomes an objectification of the devolving
history of Gold's second-generation immigrant family. The
neighborhood in which he grew up had once been a kind of
community held together by ties of blood relationship, ethnic
tradition, and loyalties growing out of the shared experience of
struggle and privation. Now the area has become a jungle and
a battlefield where teenage gangs roam the littered streets
"murdering old people casually in the course of their youthful
depredations," boarded-up shops are vandalized, and there seem
to be no places left where people can "buy food, have their suits
and dresses mended and dry cleaned, their shoes and radios fixed,
and their medical prescriptions filled." As Gold drives up
Mermaid Avenue, he does not see a single drugstore or Jewish
delicatessen. "There was no longer a movie house operating in
Coney Island: drugs, violence, and vandalism had closed both
garish, overtowering theaters years before. The brick apartment
house in which he had spent his whole childhood and nearly all
his adolescence had been razed; on the site stood something
newer and uglier that did not seem a nourishing improvement
for the Puerto Rican families there now." And Gold, like
Tiresias brooding upon the wasteland devastation, concludes:

Every good place has always been deteriorating, and everything bad is getting worse. Neighborhoods, parks, beaches, streets, schools were falling deeper into ruin and whole cities sinking into rot. . . . It was the Shoot the Chute into darkness . . . the plunging roller coaster into disintegration and squalor. Someone should do something. Nobody could. No society worth its salt would watch itself perishing without some serious attempt to avert its own destruction. Therefore . . . we are not a society. Or we are not worth our salt. Or both.

Like the old neighborhood, Gold's family once had a communal integrity founded on the need to survive in an environment that was harshly adversary not because of crime and violence but because times were hard, jobs were scarce, and too many immigrant families were competing to make a life in a new country. Gold's brother and five sisters all made large sacrifices, the brother quitting school early and going to work to help support the family, while the father lost job after job. It could hardly be said that they were happy picturesquely toiling together or even that they deeply cared for one another. They were and remained the sort of people who are caring only so long as circumstances require them to be. Now that they are middle-aged and affluent, they have disintegrated into a group of bickering malcontents who come together only because they are tyrannized into it by their maniacal 82-year-old father. At family gatherings their prime concern is to persuade him to cut short his annual visit with them and return to Florida. But he has no intention of doing so because he knows it would give them pleasure. He finds his own pleasure in abusing Gold unmercifully because Gold is an intellectual and writes articles that nobody in the family can understand and that do not make money.

All these people have long been displaced from the realities that formed them and gave them some sense of common purpose, and now they have become abstracted into caricatures of hostility and self-interest. Having survived the need to deal aggressively with their environment, they have turned their aggressions against one another, while around them what is left of their old environment is being destroyed by new generations of displaced people to whom it has no relation whatever and whose aggression against it is a means to nothing.

In the Washington sections of the novel this effect of derangement from conditions of order, sanity, and meaningful causality is achieved through a masterful burlesque of government bureaucratic life. The people in these sections are shown to be as divorced from reality as Gold's family is displaced from South Brooklyn. Political figures have lost all sense of the principles, causes, issues, and human interests they have been elected to work for and represent, and the result in their case is not aggression but a kind of psychotic arbitrariness. In the absence of clear and unavoidable imperatives that fix the nature of reality and control one's perception of it, reality can become anything one wishes it to be or decides it is. Titles of official positions have no relation to any specific function, and any office can be filled by anyone, since no one knows what qualifications are needed for what office. Therefore, any qualifications will do for any office. The language of government is similarly unrelated to the ideas or experiences it is supposed to describe. It is used not to communicate but to obscure meaning because all meaning is provisional and conjectural.

Gold hopes to be chosen for an important political position in Washington, and in an effort to win favor has written a flattering review of the President's book, *My Year in the White House*. The President, who is a pointedly unnamed successor to Gerald Ford, has evidently spent much of his first year in office writing about his first year in office. "Yet," Heller observes, "nowhere in the book does he say anything about being busy with writing the book." He is delighted with Gold's review, especially with a sentence from it, "Nothing succeeds as planned," and instructs Ralph Newsome, an old friend of Gold's now serving as an "unnamed source" in the White House, to sound him out about his interest in a government appointment. Newsome offers Gold several possible choices ranging from Ambassador to the Court of St. James's, head of NATO or the CIA, being an unnamed spokesman, Secretary of Defense, the Treasury, HEW, or the country's very first Jewish Secretary of State. ((Henry Kissinger, according to Gold, has lied about being a Jew and is really a German, perhaps even a Nazi.) Newsome assures Gold that whichever job he decides to take, he will be able to do anything he wants "as long as it's everything we tell you to say and do in support of our policies, whether you agree with them or not. You'll have complete freedom." When Gold asks for time to think all this over, Newsome tells him that "We'll want to move ahead with this as speedily as possible, although we'll have to go slowly. . . . We'll want to build this up into an important public announcement, although we'll have to be completely secret."

Gold's time in Washington is spent in repeated sessions with Newsome during which they discuss the possible jobs he might want to hold, and in trying to arrange for Gold to meet the President. But it turns out that the President actually never sees anyone and sleeps during his office hours because, as Newsome explains, "He is a very early riser. He is up at five every morning, takes two sleeping pills and a tranquilizer, and goes right back to bed for as long as he can sleep."

As he did in *Catch-22*, Heller tends here to ring too many changes on what is essentially one good joke. And the satire much of the time seems so light-heartedly outlandish that it very nearly neutralizes one's awareness that the kind of insanity Heller makes laughable has also in the real world had the most destructive consequences. Yet there is more than an edge of anger in Heller's portrait of the Washington political scene, just as there are extremely ominous implications in those general qualities of contemporary American life he has chosen to dramatize. His novel is indeed comic, often hilarously so. But it is also comedy of the bleakest and blackest kind because it is all about a society that is fast going insane, that is learning to accept chaos as order, unreality as normal. And the horror is that the time may soon come when the conditions Heller depicts will no longer seem to us either funny or the least bit odd.

William Gaddis's monumental second novel, *JR*, represents an even more ambitious effort to engage, dramatize, and ultimately burlesque the quality of anarchical derangement that seems to typify so much of the experience of our time and that Philip Roth saw as baffling and stupifying the imaginations of our novelists. *JR*, in effect, projects the condition of madness Heller envisioned in Washington bureaucracy onto the whole of society and thus faces more directly and brutally into the abyss created by the separation between language and meaning, process and purpose, and reality and reaction. But a sounder comparison may perhaps be made with *Something Happened*, where it is the unengageable benevolence of Slocum's world that is mainly responsible for his abstractedness and paranoia. If there is no reality to confront or enemies to attack, then Slocum is obliged to *create a* reality peopled with enemies who are in fact fanciful projections of his desperate need for self-confrontation. But the void in which he finds himself, and which is both out there and in him, will not be confronted. It will provide him with security and affluence, even professional success, but in all the ways that finally matter it will ignore him and thus deny him the means to test his own validity.

The situation in *JR* is rather different, but in a certain fundamental sense complementary. If Slocum is the prisoner of a dehumanized bureaucratic benevolence, Gaddis's characters are prisoners of a bureaucratic bedlam, a technology gone completely berserk, a chaos so total that within it literally anything can happen because everything is a matter of chance and the most preposterous coincidence, and the narrative form Gaddis chose is a perfect projection of this chaos.

The novel consists of 726 pages of virtually uninterrupted monologue and dialogue, an almost continuous outpouring of language embellished scarcely at all by descriptions of character and setting. People by the dozens move back and forth through thick mists of verbiage talking to and at and around and behind one another. Yet somehow nobody listens to or understands what is being said. Their milieu is as trackless and unstructured as outer space and equally crammed with junk. Debris, garbage, trash, trivia all relentlessly accumulate, even as the preoccupation of the characters is ostensibly with modes of order, classificatory arrangements, computer systems which they hope and believe will bring coherence to it all. But then we realize that these modes, and the language used to describe them, are themselves junk of another kind, semantical and technocratic quasi-structures that obscure and obfuscate rather than designate or control. And this, as it turns out, is entirely appropriate to the novel's subject—the debasement of language as both cause and symptom of the corruption of a society that has been abstracted by technology from the concrete realities of feeling and being, and in which the totalitarian prolixities of bureaucratese, the gibber and jargon of the computer, and the lying Newspeak of Watergate politics, corporate finance, and multimedia education have severed the connection that is supposed to exist between words and the truths they are intended to describe. It is a society suffering from precisely the sickness Orwell discussed in relation to political language, the decadence of which, in any culture, is a direct reflection of the decadence of thought, the need to obscure the meaning of certain politically sensitive ideas by expressing them in pseudo-scientific euphemisms or in dead metaphors that no longer have any specific evocative function. Carried far enough, this kind of semantical perversion ends in the creation of a world of fictions and forgeries in which words can be used to signify anything or nothing or are strung together to form a catechistic mumble of sounds without relation to meaning. Reality, having become whatever one wishes to name it, soon disappears behind the words employed to misname it.

Bureaucratic systems can become, as they have in our time, so intricately complex, their sources of power so diversified and mysterious, and their lines of communication so glutted with the esoteric terminology peculiar to each that they too effectively exist outside reality and cease to need any cause or objective to justify their existence. The language used to describe their operations exists, by the same token, beyond the necessity of meaning, and those who use it, as Watergate so clearly demonstrated, finally lose all sense of the moral significance of honest statement—for language is made to confuse and conceal in a situation where no one may actually know what the truth is, whether anyone anywhere is telling it, or if there is any need to do so. It is this kind of situation that Gaddis depicts with very great ingenuity, the forgeries of language in their connection with the counterfeiting of bureaucratic realities, and his emphasis is on two particular manifestations of the problem—the corporate structures of secondary education and Wall Street finance.

The action in roughly the first quarter of the novel centers in a large Long Island elementary school where several of the characters are teachers and the protagonist, JR, is an eleven-year-old sixth-grader. There is very little to indicate that any actual teaching is being done at the school because—as is the case everywhere in Gaddis's surreal projection of contemporary society—the manipulation of method, along with the complicated electronic equipment used to support it and the abstruse terminology used to mysticize it, have become ends in themselves. The function of the institution is primarily the maintenance of the institution. The teaching of students has been all but supplanted by a preoccupation with audiovisual teaching machines, public-relations problems, political strategy for obtaining foundation grants, and the allocation of funds to pay for functions that are preposterously irrelevant to the learning experience. The school budget provides $32,670 for "blacktopping the parking lot over to the TV studio," $12,000 for paper towels, $47,000 for damages resulting from vandalism, and $1200 for books for the library—an amount to be used, one character suggests, not for books but for a pegboard. "You need a pegboard in a library. Books you don't know what you're getting into." A problem heavily on the minds of the school administrators is the establishment of friendly relations with the community, and another character suggests how a school-sponsored musical program might be used to this end: "Tie it in with this culture center, locating it here, bring in your Spring Arts Festival expanded with a few remote specials stressing the patriotic theme, you might even do one on my (bomb) shelter, what America's all about, waste disposal and all, and wrap it all up with the whole in-school television program once that's on a good interference-free closed-circuit system bring in a little Foundation backing and you're on your way."

These discussions are carried on in the verbal mode that has come to dominate almost all social interchange in our time, the serial or collective monologue, and they are couched in the hieratic language of multi-media communications, in which words are used to denote conditions and processes that may be said to exist, if at all, only in the realm of the technological supernatural. One teaching method is described as being designed to "tangibilitate" certain materials. Reference is constantly being made to the "ongoing situation," someone's "position activation-wise," "motivational resource areas," and "implementing un-planlessness." One instructor says to another: "In simple straight-forward terms Dan, you might say that he structured the material in terms of the ongoing situation to tangibilitate the utilization potential of this one to one instructional medium in such a meaningful learning experience that these kids won't forget it for a hell of a long time, how's that Whiteback."

Gradually there emerges out of this babble of jargon-demented tongues the perfectly sane, merely obsessive figure of JR, logical end-product of the ongoing situation, supreme example of the utilizational potential of a meaningful learning experience. A good old American boy from his perpetually runny nose right down to his torn sneakers with the flapping soles, JR has learned his lessons well and knows by instinct how to apply them manipulatively to achieve, in the classic rags-to-riches tradition, the only goals he has been taught to respect—money, fame, and power. The one explanation he gives for his various actions is to say, "But that's what you *do*," that is what the free enterprise system requires if you expect to win, and of course everybody understands exactly what he means.

JR's interpretation of what it is you *do* to win is as central to our native ethos of self-realization as any form of adroit political or financial chicanery. Like most healthy-minded Americans he is a devout believer in the religion of technique, the *right way* to go about doing what you do that will guarantee success, and he has discovered that you can find out what the right way is by clipping coupons from the back pages of magazines and sending in for free instruction manuals along with samples of various products. In this fashion he accumulates an astounding quantity of materials including dozens of catalogues offering information on how to have meaningful sexual intercourse, how to identify rare and valuable coins, how to build powerful muscles scientifically, how to buy for practically nothing government surplus airplane gas tanks, how to get started in the import-export business, and how to make large profits by knowing the right investments to make on the stock market.

A sixth-grade field trip to Wall Street convinces JR that his destiny lies in corporation finance and, after carefully studying various pieces of free literature he has obtained from a brokerage firm, he proceeds to make an entry into the market through the purchase—entirely on paper—of thousands of Army surplus wooden picnic forks. He then becomes involved in the buying up of bankrupt companies that offer tax advantages and eventually, without at all understanding how it happened, he becomes the head of a massive conglomerate with a paper empire that includes film studios, a brewery, a firm that manufactures plastic flowers, an entire New England mill town, and a vast range of other holdings. JR conducts his business operations from a phone booth he has had installed in a corridor of his school. He muffles his voice with his handkerchief or plays a recording of his voice at a slower than normal speed to make it sound deeper. His official corporation headquarters are located in a wretched little tenement apartment on East 96th Street in Manhattan where he has installed one of his former teachers, a failed composer named Edward Bast, to pass on his instructions —which Bast cannot comprehend—and to answer the incessantly ringing telephone. The apartment is also occupied by a freaky young girl, who will sleep with absolutely anyone and when not thus engaged spends most of her time getting into and out of the bathtub, and by a weird collection of free samples, piled-up mail, and miscellaneous junk JR has sent away for. There are, among other things, thirty-six boxes of a mysterious product known as 200–2 Ply, a carton of Wise Potato Chips Hoppin' with Flavor, 24 One Pint Mazola New Improved, 24–7 oz Pkgs Flavored Loops, innumerable cans of film, volumes of Moody's *Industrials* and Thomas's *Register of American Manufacturers*, a radio buried under such a large pile of debris that no one can reach it to turn it off, a kitchen hot water faucet that also cannot be turned off, an electric clock that runs backward, and an electric letter-opener that slices letters in half. At one point a truck driver attempts to deliver a shipment of a hundred thousand plastic flowers, but is persuaded to take them back to the sender. Several men arrive with subpoenas to collect the corporation records for a governmental investigation into the legality of JR's activities, but it is by no means certain that he himself will eventually be tracked down and exposed. By the end of the novel, at any rate, he appears to be still undaunted and is last seen enthusiastically trying to con Bast into helping him launch yet another great scheme.

The absurdity of an eleven-year-old boy gaining control of a huge financial empire is the ultimate burlesque expression of an idea dramatized everywhere in this remarkable novel: that in a society such as the one depicted, absolutely anything can happen because—as Heller also indicates in a different way—no one is effectively in charge and no one can control what is going on. Certain assumptions about the fundamental coherence and value of human existence have somehow been lost. There is simply no discoverable rational structure in anything; hence, nobody makes sense either to himself or in his efforts to communicate with others. The spoken language with its endlessly reiterated ambiguities, its steady dissolution into streams of utterance signifying nothing, stands as the perfect medium for the berserk sensibility of the modern corporate state.

It is undoubtedly inevitable that the novel promises at almost every point to fall victim to the imitative fallacy, that it is frequently as turgid, monotonous, and confusing as the situation it describes. Yet Gaddis has a strength of mind and talent capable of surmounting this very large difficulty. He has managed to reflect chaos in a fiction that is not itself artistically chaotic because it is imbued with the conserving and correcting power of his imagination. His awareness of what is human and sensible is always present behind his depiction of how far we have fallen from humanity and sense. His vision of what is happening in our world is profound and deeply disturbing. If it should ever cease to disturb, there will be no better proof of its accuracy.

CHAPTER IV

Charting the Abyss

I asked them to look into the Abyss, and, both dutifully and gladly, they have looked into the Abyss, and the Abyss has greeted them with the grave courtesy of all objects of serious study, saying: "Interesting, am I not? And **exciting,** *if you consider how deep I am and what dread beasts lie at my bottom. Have it well in mind that a knowledge of me contributes materially to your being whole, or well-rounded men."*

Lionel Trilling

The view of contemporary life Don DeLillo projects in his bleak little novel, *Players*, is less complicated than Gaddis's, but equally disturbing because it illuminates yet another of the entropic processes so many writers have detected in our society. DeLillo is not concerned with the dissolution of language or the arbitrary and often hypothetical relation existing between verbal statement and rational meaning. These are clearly symptoms of what is for him the more deeply underlying disorder, the slow death of human feeling as the connections between people and the environment they move through, but do not inhabit become increasingly official and mechanical, forcing them to seek refuge from a state of external abstractedness in equally abstracting diversions and trivial games.

The chief characters of the novel are Lyle and Pammy Wynant, a bright, attractive, terribly contemporary young couple who live in a New York apartment and lead lives that appear to be typical of their class and kind. Lyle works for the Stock Exchange and Pammy for a firm called Grief Management Council, a personal-services organization that disseminates information on how to manipulate and control one's emotions so that the pain of grief will scarcely be felt at all. "There were fees for individuals, group fees, special consultation terms, charges for booklets and teaching aids, payment for family sessions and marital grief seminars." The firm is located in the World Trade Center, in which it seems to Pammy that the elevators are places and the lobbies are spaces, but the firm's presence there appears to her uncertain because office space is constantly being reapportioned. "Workmen sealed off some areas with partitions, opened up others, moved out file cabinets, wheeled in chairs and desks. It was as though they'd been directed to adjust the amount of furniture to levels of national grief."

Pammy and Lyle do their jobs with robotic efficiency, she writing promotional literature for the firm, he trading on the floor of the Exchange. But both are totally abstracted from their places of work and can find no meaning in their functions. At the Exchange, Lyle diverts himself by imagining that everyone knows his thoughts and is aware that they consist of "unword-able rubble, the glass, rags and paper of his tiny indefinable manias." While walking in the streets he has a compulsive habit of putting together physical descriptions of people and of memorizing the numbers on license plates—as if he were preparing to be interrogated by the police at the scene of a crime. Pammy at work is obsessed with the unclassifiable nature of her surroundings. "If the elevators were places . . . and the lobbies were spaces . . . what then was the World Trade Center itself? Was it a condition, an occurrence, a physical event, an existing circumstance, a presence, a state, a set of variables?" Lyle, by contrast, feels that he is present only in *things*. "There was more of him here through the idle nights than he took home with him to vent and liberate. He thought about the nights. He imagined the district never visited, empty of human transaction, and how buildings such as these would seem to hold untouchable matter, enormous codifications of organic decay. He tried to examine the immense complexity of going home."

When not at work Lyle and Pammy follow a routine that has grown steadily more autistic.

> They used to spend a lot of time discovering restaurants. They traveled to the palest limits of the city, eating in little river warrens near the open approaches to bridges or in family restaurants out in the boroughs, the neutral decor of such places and their remoteness serving as tokens of authenticity. They went to clubs where new talent auditioned and comic troupes improvised. On spring weekends they bought plants at greenhouses in the suburbs and went to boatyards on City Island or the North Shore to help friends get their modest yachts seaworthy. Gradually their range diminished. Even movies, double features in the chandeliered urinals of upper Broadway, no longer tempted them. What seemed missing was the desire to compile.
>
> They had sandwiches for dinner, envelopes of soup, or went around the corner to a coffee shop. . . . There was a Chinese place three blocks away. This was as far as they traveled, most evenings and weekends.

Lyle passes the time at night watching television, but turns the channel selector every minute or so because he is interested only in "jerking the dial into fresh image-burns." Pammy putters around the apartment, thinking on one occasion that she should feel like eating fruit, which she constantly buys and leaves to rot in the refrigerator. But "she couldn't deal with the consequences of fruit, its perishability, the duty involved in eating it. She wanted to sit in a corner, alone, and stuff herself with junk." When now and then they make love, they do so with small lust and less affection, and Lyle is conscious throughout that "it is time to 'perform.' . . . She would have to be 'satisfied.' He would have to 'service' her. They would make efforts to 'interact.' "

Two occurrences dislodge the Wynants from their catatonia, one initiated by violence, the other resulting in violence, and both are attractive to them because they promise to open a way to feeling and adventure and offer at least momentary escape from an existence that is completely without point. But in the process of becoming involved, the Wynants come to seem malevolent because their involvement is nothing more than irresponsible play-acting in a melodrama of real life in which the participants may be injured or killed and genuine consequences have to be faced.

Lyle's involvement begins when an acquaintance of his, a fellow stockbroker, is shot on the floor of the Exchange. It is a scene reminiscent of Heller: a man is shot; nobody knows why. But the mystery titillates Lyle, and it happens that through a woman with whom he is having a totally bloodless affair, he is able to become part of it. The woman introduces him to a group of terrorists who are plotting to blow up the Exchange and who had been using the dead man as an inside accomplice. For no reason other than the fact that he thinks the experience might make life real to him, Lyle volunteers to take the dead man's place. He is last seen in Canada waiting in a motel for a phone call that will give him instructions on just what part he will play in the conspiracy. But the novel ends, and the phone does not ring. "He decides to count to one hundred. If the phone doesn't ring at one hundred, his instinct has deceived him, the pattern has cracked, his waiting has opened out to magnitudes of gray space. He will pack and leave. One hundred is the outer margin of his passive assent."

While Lyle is thus engaged, Pammy takes a vacation in Maine with two male homosexual friends whom she and Lyle have always found amusing. After spending several days with them in an isolated cabin she slowly perceives that their relationship, which she had assumed to be cheerfully casual, is actually compounded of deep hostility and jealousy, although for Jack, the younger of the two, it is quite literally all that holds his life together. As the relationship deteriorates, Jack turns in desperation to Pammy, and she, out of curiosity and boredom, has intercourse with him. Whether or not as a result of this, Jack grows increasingly despondent and shortly thereafter is discovered to have committed suicide by covering himself with gasoline and setting himself afire.

This is a kind of reality Pammy cannot bear. She has drifted irresponsibly into what has become a fatal involvement in other people's lives, and that fact very nearly destroys the thin detachment that preserves her from the world. So she retreats to the sanctuary of the apartment where her nullity has become institutionalized in small protective rituals, and she can return to viewing other people as safely alien phenomena.

The novel's opening scene brilliantly pantomimes the theme the subsequent action develops. A young couple—obviously Lyle and Pammy—are sitting in the piano bar of an airliner. In the forward seating area a film is being shown, but since they have no headsets, the people in the bar are unable to hear the soundtrack. However, the pianist improvises a parodistic nickelodeon score for the silent action on the screen, expertly shifting rhythm and mood to suit the growing ominousness of what is taking place.

> Golfers plod on screen, seven or eight in all, white, male, portly, several driving golf carts, bumping slowly over knolls in single file. They're all middle-aged and wear the kind of rampantly bright sports clothes that suburban men favor on weekends, colors so strident they might serve as illustrations of the folly of second childhood.

But then "a man . . . rises from the underbrush in the immediate foreground. . . . When he turns to signal to someone, it's evident he holds a weapon in his right hand, a semiautomatic rifle." The golfers come under savage attack by terrorists and are quickly shot or run down and hacked to death with machetes—all to the accompaniment of the sardonic burlesque of the piano music, which has the effect finally of nullifying the horrors enacted on the screen and relegating them to the emotionally neutral dimension of media melodrama.

> To the glamour of revolutionary violence, to the secret longing it evokes in the most docile soul, the piano's shiny tinkle brings an irony too apt to be ignored. The simple innocence of this music undermines the photogenic terror, reducing it to an empty swirl. . . . We're prompted to remem-

ber something here . . . a spool of Biograph dreams . . . upright
pianos in a thousand nickelodeons. Heart-throbbing romance
and knock-about comedy and nerve-racking suspense. History
this weightless has an easy time of it, we learn, contending with
the burdens of the present day.

The scene not only foreshadows the Wynants' subsequent
involvement with, in Lyle's case, conspiratorial terrorism and,
in Pammy's, with the violence of Jack's suicide, but it also
dramatizes the condition of mind that makes such involvement
possible. The actions of the terrorists occur in the only medium
in which most people witness violence, the safely distanced and
vicariously experienced medium of film or television. Yet such
is the nature of the detachment imposed by these media that
the depicted violence seems more real than real life, which is
often so insulated against aggressive action that it seems totally
unreal and unengageable. This is the Wynants' situation. They
must try to find in actual experience the excitement media
violence creates in them, for they assume that if it is that exciting
vicariously, it must be far more exciting when one participates
directly in it. But at a time when so much that happens in the
public world is a theatrical performance or a demonstration put
on for the purposes of media publicity, one might also conclude
that all violent actions are more theatrical than real. Thus, the
Wynants, in trying to find a life that will make them feel alive,
seek out extreme and dangerous situations, mistaking the media
version for real life. They become "players" in what is for them
a stage production, but the "act" in their case is violent actuality.

However gratuitous their behavior may be, the terrorists
function to make objective and concrete the otherwise undocu-
mented effect of generalized conspiracy that pervades the
Wynants' story and that can be felt in so much of our contemporary fiction. They offer a promise of order and intelligible,
if misdirected purpose in an environment in which the sources
of power seem mysterious and unreachable, and the consequences
of individual action exist without relation to any context of
judgment that might give them emotional or moral meaning.

This, one finally perceives, will be the result of the Wynants' efforts to be caught up in experiences that will make them feel real. No matter what the physical outcome may be—whether Lyle finds martyrdom as a terrorist or Pammy through Jack's death a momentary confrontation with the fact of evil—in the end nothing will have changed for them or within them. They will remain dead to themselves because, although they have been acted upon by powers of conspiracy and evil, they have never possessed, and do not come to possess, the redeeming powers of compassion and will.

In much of the fiction of Jerzy Kosinski one finds an exactly opposite situation. His novels cannot be called narratives of action in the conventional sense nor are they chronicles of character development. In fact, it would seem fair to say that in nearly all of them there is no development of any kind, no accumulation of history, no dimension of sequential time, no before or after, only a series of moments suspended in space without precedent and without consequence.

Except for *Being There*, which represents a distinct departure from his other work, Kosinski's novels record isolated and unconnected instances of the often brutal display of personal power in a social milieu so empty of content that what few characters there are float within it without being acted upon by any force other than their own obsessions. Like the Wynants they are all creatures of the contemporary void. But where the Wynants occupy an environment whose only relation to them is its abstracting lack of relation, the environment of Kosinski's characters simply cannot be said to exist. Hence, it is the compulsive function of his protagonists—all of whom are solitary males—to try to counter and repopulate the prevailing nullity by creating elaborate intrigues and melodramas, the sole purpose of which is to display the protagonists' power to manipulate, control, torment, and punish other people, to substitute for the moral anarchy of the void the autocracy of personal law, the tyranny of the imperious self.

To achieve his ends the Kosinski protagonist makes use of various disguises and impersonations, electronic devices and technological strategms—all the methods of modern terrorism put to the service of the lone assassin. For he is the master of a world in which anything can happen and anybody—namely himself—can with enough ruthlessness and cunning *make* anything happen. In distinct contrast to the novels of Heller and Gaddis, in which the characters feel that their lives are being acted upon and shaped by the sinister forces of a world gone berserk, that powers beyond reason and comprehension seem to be in control, perhaps through conspiratorial design, perhaps through cosmic accident or caprice, Kosinski's fiction has to do with the seizure of *personal* control—again with terrorist bravado —just because the structures of control that might have prevented such seizure or made it unnecessary have collapsed in society at large.

The experience of Kosinski's first protagonist, the young boy of *The Painted Bird*, established the emotional pattern of all his successors except Chance in *Being There*. They are all scarred and lone survivors in a world to which their responses have been frozen by the unbelievable horrors of the boy's persecution at the hands of brutish peasants during his years of wandering in Nazi-occupied Poland. Any one of them might have come out of Dachau or Auschwitz—and, indeed, that is the experience to which the boy's suffering is evidently meant to stand as metaphor. But unlike most such survivors they have been infected with a single demonic compulsion: to take revenge upon the human race by inflicting punishment even more gratuitous and terrible than any suffered by the boy.

Thus it is that these black knights or agents of retribution— some quite literally secret, double, and/or CIA—wander up and down a world that is a projection of the nightmarish landscape of wartime Poland. They are as alone as the boy, but they are no longer defenseless. Obsessive to the point of catatonia, they come to full awareness of the life outside themselves only when they recognize situations which threaten them or in which they can become threatening, or when they encounter people who appear deserving of their intricately plotted schemes for torment and humiliation. Nothing else attracts or seems worthy of their attention except certain sexual opportunities for which they have a bizarre and sadistic appetite.

In some respects Kosinski's typical protagonist closely resembles Georges Poulet's Marivaudian being who is described by Donald Barthelme in *Unspeakable Practices, Unnatural Acts* as "a pastless futureless man, born anew at every instant. The instants are points which organize themselves into a line, but what is important is the instant, not the line. The Marivaudian being has in a sense no history. Nothing follows from what has gone before. He is constantly surprised. He cannot predict his own reaction to events. He is constantly being *overtaken* by events." The difference of course is that in his pastless and futureless condition Kosinski's protagonist is never surprised and is only initially overtaken by events. The moment he sees an opportunity for revenge and persecution, he becomes a *shaper* of events and causes events, usually horrible, to overtake other people—these becoming the principal, if not the sole ingredients of action in his extended story.

Since he operates alone, entirely without accomplices, the protagonist must rely, as I have said, upon subterfuge and technology to aid him in his deadly work, and he has trained himself to become expert in the use of a wide array of mechanisms, all of which are cunningly designed to maim or destroy without revealing the identity of the destroyer. He will construct a lethal machine for any nefarious purpose, plant a bomb to be electronically detonated on a crowded Alpine cable car, arrange for an uncooperative girlfriend to be exposed to a fatal dose of radiation from the radar system of a military jet, or, without the help of technology, he will have her gang-raped by a group of diseased and filthy Bowery bums he has carefully recruited for the occasion.

The protagonist performs these actions quite mechanically, seemingly with little satisfaction, and totally without remorse. They appear to be ritual gestures or ceremonial sacrifices made in a social milieu so completely lacking in the public ingredients of ceremony that they seem to carry their own defiant justification—as if through the violence done to others some lost principle of order or rationality were affirmed or redeemed, as if gratuitous evil, no matter the degree of its horror, were infinitely preferable to the moral nullity in which it is made to occur. Kosinski seems constantly in his fiction to be trying to authenticate Eliot's observation that "so far as we are human, what we do must be either evil or good; so far as we do evil or good, we are human; and it is better, in a paradoxical way, to do evil than to do nothing: at least we exist. . . . The worst that can be said of most of our malefactors, from statesmen to thieves, is that they are not men enough to be damned."

Perhaps it is one of Kosinski's more exemplary intentions to try to reconstitute the reality of evil and the risk of damnation. But the problem remains that since there exists in his fiction no adversary dimension of good, no decorum of virtue that evil violates and thus becomes a heresy, the actions of his protagonists, while clearly evil by moral standards the reader may bring to the fiction, take place in a context altogether devoid of standards by which they might be morally judged and condemned.* Hence, what they seem to dramatize—and perhaps are actually meant to dramatize—is the meaninglessness of even the most horrendous actions when perpetrated in a condition of such moral impotence that they are finally placed beyond judgment and rendered unworthy of damnation. Kosinski's protagonists may not be men enough to be damned. But if they are not, the fault may not lie in them but in the world they inhabit, the terribly contemporary world that has lost the power of damnation in its zeal to explain the inexplicable and forgive the unspeakable. Should that prove to be true, we may have here yet another of the many examples to be found in current literature of what happens when fiction attempts to become a direct reflection of the void and so risks becoming a statement about emptiness which is itself empty.

At some point in any consideration of what Kosinski seems to

---

* Raskolnikov's situation in *Crime and Punishment* is a strikingly different case in point. As I described it in an earlier essay, "We are able to appreciate the enormity of his crime and . . . the anguish of his guilt because the crime comes to us in the context of the morality which it violates, just as the guilt comes to us in the context of the morality out of which it derives. It is the material of participation and judgment which the novel provides through the ingredients of character, scene, and sensory language, rather than the material . . . we bring with us into the novel out of life, that affords us our angle of vision, that enables us to *see* into Raskolnikov and to assess both his crime and the quality of his conscience."

be trying to do, the question must arise as to whether his work can best be understood as parable based largely on personal fantasy or as a kind of gothically distorted, but nonetheless realistically intended rendering of actual experience. One finds it very difficult to decide whether he should be read as Kafka and perhaps Céline should be read—that is, with large allowances for their pathological aberrations of vision—or whether he is simply raising to the highest conceivable demonic power the products of his essentially quite sane vision of the way contemporary life is actually being lived.

Surely, his fiction appears to have much to say about the pervasive need in our time to manufacture structures, systems, strategies, and roles that will provide a coherence, however diabolical, in which human actions can achieve dramatic significance and the relations among people will take on at least the interest of psychological tension and conflict. He also seems to have understood the enormous power we have vested in technology as the ultimate weapon of manipulation and domination in a society possessing few more basic means by which influence upon others can be exercised. And of course behind his view of technology there is the perception that a mechanical and pitiless hostility embodied in and symbolized by the machine lies at the center of such a significant part of contemporary human relationship. The need to force others to do one's bidding in the face of this hostility creates a warfare of wills that can be won only through the most adroit and unremitting management of the techniques of persuasion. The roles one assumes are perhaps the most potent of those techniques because they represent a fictitious identity created for a particular occasion in order to give the role-player the advantage of altogether false pretenses with which to mould the occasion to suit his personal ends. Life thus becomes a work of art, a masquerade ball, a game of Russian roulette—whatever one has sufficient ingenuity to make seem real. And this is possible only when other means of creating and validating reality have suffered a massive loss of authority.

All these and other suggestions that Kosinski is seeking to comment in his oblique way on existing social and moral conditions are to be found in his work. But there is still the problem that his presentation of them is *so* oblique that the distinction between personal fantasy and realistic portraiture can never be clearly drawn, nor does the effectiveness of the fantasy as a symbol of life in our time appear unquestionable. Between the symbol and the condition of life falls a shadow of more than ambiguity, perhaps of temperamental perverseness, perhaps of a failure, surely not of nerve, but of compassion.

Every serious writer among us is seeking a form that will, again to quote Eliot, give "a shape and a significance to the immense panorama of futility and anarchy which is contemporary history." Kosinski has clearly responded to the futility and anarchy. But his dark fables mirror them without shaping their significance. The reason may be that he has found none and is saying so.

CHAPTER V

Mere Entropy Is Loosed

Thomas Pynchon's own monumental effort to create shape and significance and so make contemporary history possible for art has led him to formulate a metaphysics derived not from the world of human affairs, but from the technology of science. Since the beginning of his career Pynchon has been obsessed with essentially one idea and its manifold permutations, the idea that the universe—and by strong implication modern society—is in a state of slow disintegration because of an irreversible loss of energy through the process of entropy as defined by the second and third laws of thermodynamics. According to these laws, a gradual but inexorable leveling of energy is occurring throughout the universe in response to the tendency of a thermodynamic system to move from the least probable to the most probable molecular distribution, from a state of molecular organization capable of producing work to a state of random, uniform molecular action. At the end of the entropic process, heat energy, which must pass from a hot object to a colder one, will no longer be transferable because everything will contain an equal amount of energy or have reached the same degree of temperature. As Henry Adams, to whom Pynchon owes much, also saw, the force of entropy has increased throughout history; the world is moving inevitably and ever more rapidly toward its extinction. Diversity in both the universe and the human social order is giving way to homogeneity, purposeful and productive action to arbitrary randomness, life-affirming moral system to the technological death-system—the animate to the inanimate.

Against the threat of dissolution posed by the force of entropy Pynchon raises certain provisional structures of coherence that promise to provide some means of comprehending experiences that seem to occur randomly and outside the stabilizing logic of cause and effect. One such structure is founded on the notion of worldwide or perhaps even cosmic conspiracy, the existence of a massive and mysterious system devoted to the secret manipulation of persons and events so that they can be made to serve the unknown ambitions of those in power. According to Pynchon, humankind has been engaged in creating systems ever since the first men confronted the wilderness and found its apparent formlessness unbearable. The imposition of a concept of order, however specious or exploitative its purposes may be, became the psychic necessity of the race, just as paranoia, the belief in conspiracy, became its dominant psychic disease, one that has reached epidemic proportions in the modern age, particularly with the triumph of electronic technology after World War II. Unlike Kosinski's protagonists who, in the absence of received systems of collective moral order, impose their personal power upon others through conspiratorial systems they seem arbitrarily to invent for the diabolical occasion, Pynchon invests power in bureaucratic organizations that are very probably malevolent, that command vast wealth and technology and that are directed by scientists and international cartel tycoons—power so invested being for him the prime force for good or evil in a period of history that lacks or has lost all other means of giving moral shape and direction to human existence.

The major characters of Pynchon's three novels—Herbert Stencil in *V*, Oedipa Maas in *The Crying of Lot 49*, and Tyrone Slothrop in *Gravity's Rainbow*—are all obsessed with the idea of conspiracy and determined to expose its workings and the identities of those in control. Their effort to discern the lineaments of plot, to decide whether everything is, in fact, connected with everything else, may or may not be an expression of their paranoia. But the effort provides them with a certain—perhaps their only—coherence and substance as characters and prevents them from lapsing into randomness and anti-paranoia (the fate of those for whom nothing seems to be connected with anything) and finally into a state of inertia, in which one becomes an inanimate object or a thing, like the elusive V. whom Stencil forever pursues and who becomes increasingly a creature of prosthentic attachments as her story develops until at the end she is more metal and plastic than flesh.

In Pynchon's world one can either seek endlessly and futilely to expose conspiracy and achieve purpose in the search or, somewhat paradoxically, one can struggle to avoid becoming inanimate by keeping oneself in a constant state of randomness, resisting all emotional commitments, all roles and relations that might force one to function within a single specific identity—as, for example, Benny Profane does in *V.*, a character who cannot live in peace with inanimate objects and whose relation to life is epitomized by his habit of spending days yo-yoing or shuttling on the subway "back and forth underneath 42nd Street, from Times Square to Grand Central and vice versa." But in either case, the result is ambiguous. Those bent on exposing conspiracy not only do not expose it, they are unable even to find it. Those committed to maintaining their identities in randomness become imprisoned in that condition, remain forever in movement like Profane, or ultimately lose identity and just fade away. In fact, Pynchon's novels—particularly *Gravity's Rainbow*—tend to exemplify in their form the philosophy they expound: their dramatic pattern is itself a correlative of the entropic process. They begin typically with the creation of an effect or paranoid delusion of conspiracy, with an impression of coherence and control created by the supposed existence of conspiratorial plan. Then as the search for it deepens and the seekers become steadily more frustrated, the precarious structuring of the fiction begins to collapse, scenes of capricious or inexplicable behavior, bizarre cartoonographic characters and situations come to dominate the action—until finally both the action and the characters dissolve into randomness and often, like Slothrop near the end of *Gravity's Rainbow*, seem to disappear altogether.

There can be no doubt that Pynchon possesses a major literary intelligence, perhaps the finest mind to appear in our literature since Henry James. But Pynchon is clearly not a major novelist—if, that is, we are still permitted to measure the worth of a novelist by the depth of his perception of human character and sensibility. Pynchon's deficiency in this respect appears to stem from the fact that, unlike James, his mind, however fine, has been thoroughly violated by an idea, and one that is drastically unsuited to expression in the novel form. The plain truth is that human beings are not explainable nor are they governable by the laws that define the activities of heat molecules or the chemical structure of carbon rings. To assume that they are is inevitably to treat them as if they had no free will, no power of self-determination, no control over their environment, no emotional or ethical substance, and no individual dignity—to reduce them, in short, to interchangeable ciphers or phenomenological data programmed by a computer. But then Pynchon is concerned not with the drama and mystery of life, but rather with its ultimate and unavoidable extinction in entropic chaos, which is perhaps to say that the human situation seems to him irrelevant or trivial when viewed from the perspective of the cosmos and when the fate of life is already a foregone conclusion. He is thus a kind of apocalyptic naturalist who sees temporal experience as having meaning only in relation to its transcendental implications or only as it represents one barely significant aspect of universal process. He does, to be sure, attempt to come to terms with all those baleful preoccupations we have come to associate with the modern dilemma—the prevailing sense of imminent catastrophe and worldwide conspiracy, our obsession with technology, bureaucracy, espionage, terrorism, consciousness-raising and the occult, sexual perversion, self-perfection, and death. And these are concerns that do provide a source of potential drama for the novelist at a time when the social and moral imperatives, those created by religion and class, which once defined and directed human behavior, have lost their force. But Pynchon is unable to make the laws of chemistry and physics into plausible substitutes for human law because their connection to the fate of individual people simply cannot be determined or dramatized.

All this seems a pity for there is evidence throughout his work that Pynchon is capable of much more. In fact, whenever he begins to blunder into the precincts of the novel of social realism, he may go on for a time creating magnificently believable characters and situations. But then, as if through the exercise of sheer will, he forces himself back into an elaboration and attenuation of his entropic view of existence, turning resolutely away, as the good descendant of Puritans that he is, from the knowledge his blunder has demonstrated—that there are still living people out there, that they have emotions, dreams, and difficulties in a world that, although it may be dying, is still their only world, and that the character and behavior of the living is the first concern of the novelist, not the process of death.

CHAPTER VI

The Banality of Evil

But then abstract ideas about the nature of life or death have almost always been poorly served in the American novel. We have had, to be sure, many works of high rhetorical pretentiousness, crowded with the vividly rendered life of raw experience, promising significance on every page, but seldom delivering anything very much weightier than the accrued poundage of their pages. We have had other works of great lyrical intensity and still others of the most corrosive social criticism and satire, in which we may learn all about the distresses and stupidities of American life, but almost nothing about what it means.

Our novels have usually lacked what the best of European fiction has traditionally possessed in abundance: the power to deal directly with abstract concepts of being and to depict ideas as concrete modes of dramatic action to be experienced with all the force of physical sensations. For reasons that may derive from the peculiarities of our national history and psychology, American novelists have rarely been able to extrapolate from the immediate and local predicaments of their characters to the general human truths they may typify—in the way, for example, that Flaubert could create out of the tragedy of one bored provincial housewife a universal portrait of the bourgeois mind, or Dostoevsky out of the sufferings of a poor student a classic study of the psychology of guilt, or Tolstoy out of the disparate lives of some Russian aristocrats the history of an entire epoch. We have had *The Scarlet Letter*, but no *Madame Bovary* or *Crime and Punishment*, *Moby-Dick*, but no *War and Peace*—we have had novels, that is, possessing a certain kind of greatness, but their significance so often seems confined, even when they strain for allegorical generalization, within the limits of the particular situations they dramatize. The result is that they finally seem to be about merely personal guilt rather than the force of evil, merely individual failure rather than the tragedy of human existence. It is possible that American novelists are by nature limited to the specific and particular, that they have sensations or at best perceptions instead of ideas, and that they write most convincingly when they are absolved of the obligation of having to think.

Part of our problem may be that the Puritan settlers arrived in this country with such a bleak and negative attitude toward experience that, while it may have equipped them admirably to endure hardship, it also helped to impoverish both the realistic and the intellectual content of American fiction throughout its formative years. In the Puritan view, experience of this world represented temptation to sinful indulgence and wherever possible was to be resisted so that the soul might be properly prepared for its sojourn in the City of God. Eternal life in the hereafter was the reward for renunciation of the enticements of this life. As a result of this doctrine, our fiction writers for many years were beset by such a fear of secular reality that most of them very nearly managed to eliminate it from their work altogether and devoted themselves to dramatizing, on the transcendental plane of allegory and theological romance safely removed from corruptive actuality, what were essentially versions of the Puritan struggle for salvation.

This may help to explain why Hawthorne and Melville seem so deficient in a sense of social fact. Their imaginative eye seems always to be fixed on the cosmos, and their novels give the effect of taking place in a sanctified vacuum virtually uncontaminated by the presence of people. The thinness of the human and social scene in Hawthorne is so obtrusive that it is itself almost a presence, and perhaps fortunately for Melville *Moby-Dick* had logically to take place at sea, so that there would be minimal worldly intrusions on Ahab's solipsistic battle with the brute force of evil nature.

It is of course true—and it has often been said—that in

comparison with Europe the social scene in the America of their time *was* thin. That is an important reason for their preoccupation with romance and allegory and, in Hawthorne's case, the Puritan past. But it is also why our early writers had such difficulty creating thematic meanings that would have some generalizing relation to the human condition as a whole. The wonderfully complicated network of family and national history, political intrigue, traditions of place and creed, titled aristocracy, and institutionalized peasantry that created the rich texture of European life and literature simply did not exist for them, and in addition to Hawthorne, at least two other classic American fiction writers—Cooper and James—made regretful public acknowledgment of the fact.

But as the country expanded westward after the Civil War, it became evident that American life was developing a character quite unlike the European, but capable of providing vital materials for the many writers who were eager to declare their independence from both Europe and the Puritan past. The defining feature of that character was linear movement in geographic space, the exploration of unknown territory, the effort to discover and absorb vast new areas of raw experience. It is not surprising that the sternly renunciatory Puritan attitude toward experience could not survive in a nation passionately committed to embracing experience. But what did happen was that the force of Puritan spirituality was diverted from the transcendent to the secular, and in the process the secular was spiritualized. Physical experience became sacramental, and our literature came to treat the quest for salvation in experience with the kind of shrill religiosity once reserved for the soul's quest for salvation in Heaven.

Whitman and James both saw experience in this way, as spiritually redemptive, as a mystical boon to be sought through embracing multitudes or, as Lambert Strether says in James's *The Ambassadors*, through living all you can—as if immersion in life were the gateway to Godhead. And so evidently it seemed to many of the American writers who came after them. They formed a priestly cult of worshippers at the shrine of experience, and each in his way made his pilgrimage down the road to some earthly New Jerusalem that was located just beyond the next range of mountains or across the Atlantic Ocean or just about anywhere promising escape from the barren, oppressive towns in which they grew up. Some became insatiable consumers of the Eucharist of merely additive living, great chunks of which came out half-digested in their books because they were governed by no conviction that experience in fiction was supposed to *mean*: its justification lay in the miraculous fact of its having happened. An abstract thought or idea was a threat to the integrity of raw sensation, a blasphemy on the sacredness of pure actuality. It is no accident that even T.S. Eliot, the most cerebral of our poets, could observe of even James, the most cerebral of our novelists, that he "had a mind so fine that no idea could violate it," that famous remark that undoubtedly referred to James's vast non-denominational sensibility, but that might also be interpreted, given the choice of words, as a compliment to James on his having successfully protected his intellectual virginity against despoliation by a rapine idea.

Thomas Wolfe was of course the classic case of the American novelist bent on chasing down and eating up the whole of human experience. But Wolfe's subject was finally merely himself in the act of chasing down and eating up, and his effort to give significance to that act found expression in a wild sentimentality of language that sought its vindication in the inflations of its rhetoric, but remained unredeemed by a single idea. Hemingway's contribution to the intellectual enrichment of the American novel consisted of his discovery that "morals are what you feel good after." Fitzgerald, who had by far the better mind, had certain subtler perceptions about the meaning of moral conduct. But his villains and villainesses were more emptily careless or simply spoiled than they were evil, while his heroes were too naïve or weak to be heroic. Dos Passos had what might be called an idea of American society—that it was dominated and dehumanized by an exploitative capitalist system—but the idea ultimately hardened into an ideology and ossified his vision.

In more recent times, with the Western frontier long closed and the more obvious features of American life thoroughly defined in fiction, our writers have sought to appease their hunger for new imaginative frontiers through an exploration of the internal wilderness of their own psyches, out of which some like Roth, Bellow, and Heller have produced, as I have said, a fictional form that has become characteristic of our time: the novel of vociferous *external* monologue in which the voice of the protagonist is the only important character and his paranoia frequently the only substance. Other writers have executed an inward turning, not into the psyche, but into the technical resources of the fictional form itself, seeking to find in their experiments with myth, fable, self-parody, and the uses of fictions and non-fictions within fictions some means of creating systems of order and significance in a period of our history that seems to possess little or none. They have perhaps been most successful in producing book-length seriocomic metaphors of contemporary experience, in which they are often able to express the idea—as Pynchon does—that all life is dying, mere entropy is loosed upon the world, or that no idea is tenable as a program for living, as John Barth keeps saying in various ways, or that life is so absurd that one's only hope of remaining sane is to resort to cute little incantations of adolescent stoicism—"So it goes" and "hi ho," Kurt Vonnegut's idea so banal that no mind could possibly want to violate it.

William Styron's problem is not so much that he is unable to express his ideas through his fiction as that he seems not to have ideas to express. Like Thomas Wolfe, the literary predecessor he most closely resembles, Styron has a natural story-teller's gift for concocting enormous quantities of narrative material, but he has the greatest difficulty finding ways to make his material meaningful. This has been particularly burdensome for Styron because, while there is little to indicate that he is a writer struggling to express a major vision of life, he has all along given the appearance of being a writer driven by the most intense ambition to be *considered* major, and he knows that to achieve this he must appear to possess major themes. He seems, therefore, to have tried to assimilate into his work elements conventionally associated with the presence of something important to say. He writes in a style that has come to be identified, at least in more conservative literary circles, as the traditional style of our native form of important fiction. It is grandly rhetorical, seemingly always portentous of some large cosmic or apocalyptic significance, rich with atmospheric perfume, swollen with adjectival bloat, and most effective when it is at work on the experience of the South as previously processed by the imagination of William Faulkner.

Styron's dramatic situations are also those indemnified by past usage as serious and important. He is particularly infatuated with situations that lend themselves to the fullest epical or sentimental orchestration, that will resonate most forebodingly with deep tonalities of disaster and doom—murder, suicide, insanity, rape, incest, miscegenation, ancestral blood-guilt, generalized corruption and betrayal, the kinds of materials that served Faulkner so well just because they were inseparable from the cultural and moral derangement of his Southern characters. But in Styron's handling of them they seem to exist for their own sake or the sake of mere theatrics without relation to the thematic meaning they are ostensibly designed to express. They constantly generate promises of meaning far larger than the capacity of his characters to fulfill them.

But Styron has recognized that to be considered major a writer must not only appear to be engaging major themes. He must also engage them at the right time, when the public for one reason or another will find them topically important or intellectually fashionable. Thus, by strategy or accident, he published his widely praised first novel, *Lie Down in Darkness*, in 1952, at just the moment when it could be read as the final flowering of the Southern novel after Faulkner, a brilliant synthesis of all the elements of Southern fiction at the culmination of its renaissance following World War II. The fact that most of these elements had by this time hardened into stereotypes actually worked in Styron's favor because it enabled general readers to admire the novel for qualities they could readily recognize as belonging to an established literary tradition, but one which had ceased long ago to disturb them with original thought.

Something rather different occurred with the appearance in 1960 of Styron's second novel, *Set This House on Fire*, a massive, meandering work that was heavily swathed in the costumery of would-be majorness and that appeared to represent an effort to exploit trendy highbrow interests, perhaps in order to win the favor of the many intellectuals who had disdained *Lie Down in Darkness* because it was so mechanically derivative of Faulkner. In particular, Styron tried to give coherence and meaning to his endlessly attenuated story, which had to do with some troubled people involved in a mysterious murder case, through windy adumbrations of existential *Angst*, the Big Questions about "being" and "nothingness" that Sartre and Camus had a good while before made fashionable. But by the time Styron finished the novel—and he writes very slowly—the fashion had passed, and the intellectuals whose good will the book seemed intended to court savaged it for being out-of-date as well as for shamming a significance it did not and could not deliver.

By contrast, the publication of *The Confessions of Nat Turner*, in 1967, nicely coincided with the furor then being generated by the Civil Rights movement. But Styron's error in that novel was political as well as artistic. His portrait of slave-insurrectionist Turner infuriated many black writers because it seemed to them the height of arrogance for a Southern white to disregard many important facts about Turner's life and character and produce a fictionalized account that not only distorted the truth but was clearly racist in point of view. Nevertheless, the book was sensational and titillating enough to survive the controversy, and it became the most commercially successful of Styron's novels up to that time.

When he conceived the plan for his most recent novel, *Sophie's Choice*, Styron could well have had grounds for believing that this time there was absolutely no way he could lose. He had chosen as his central subject the most calamitous event of modern history, the systematic murder of Nazi concentration camp inmates, and he could be reasonably certain that interest in the Holocaust would persist no matter how long it took him to finish the book. He also had some fat chunks of Southern experience, which, when heated up by his prose, could be counted on to generate the atmosphere of gaseous gloom and fatality on which the flavor of his work depends. And he had in addition the story of his own early years as a writer when he was struggling to write the book that became *Lie Down in Darkness*, was fired from his job with McGraw-Hill for floating plastic bubbles out of a window on the 20th floor of their building, and was devoting the rest of his time to trying, in the lust of his virginal frustration, to get as many women into bed as he possibly could—an effort that failed repeatedly but that yielded some fairly savory anecdotal material.

Styron also had a somewhat shopworn, but nonetheless great potential theme, the question of responsibility for the Nazi atrocities and in particular the guilt of those who survived them, a theme certified to be great by important thinkers like Hannah Arendt, Bruno Bettelheim, and George Steiner and others whom Styron takes care to cite in his narrative, especially when they offer him free insurance against criticism by remarking on just how difficult it would be for a writer to make such a theme dramatically convincing. But putting it all together, Styron had the makings of a rich heavy brew that seemed guaranteed to give off the aroma of grand significance for a good while to come.

As he did in his previous novels, Styron tries in *Sophie's Choice* to create suspense by resorting to the form of the detective story, a form well suited to the writer who wishes to explore a complicated mystery to its ingenious solution, but can also be adapted to the purposes of a writer seeking to generate a counterfeit effect of complication out of materials that are in themselves so shallow that he can imagine no other way of making them seem significant. Styron's strategy is to gather together great masses of material having to do with people whose behavior seems strange or inexplicable and then scrutinize every last scrap of information about them as if it were a vital clue to a puzzle he holds himself interminably on the point of being about to solve. This involves him in an activity that he obviously enjoys above all other things and that most vividly demonstrates his quality as a writer: the dogged documentation of absolutely everything, the creation of vast marathon descriptions that go on and on for hundreds of pages and always have behind them the implication that some wondrous profundity will at any moment be divulged to a stunned world.

In the opening sections of the novel we are introduced to

Stingo, Styron's narrator-persona, a character seemingly without thematic relevance to the main action but whose presence in the novel may be justified by the fact that Styron appears to have wanted to work his early literary and sexual experiences into the story, and at the same time had need of a narrator. The suspenseful questions about Stingo are whether he will manage without regular income to keep going as a writer and whether he will finally find a woman who will relieve him of his virginity. Styron is able to protract an examination of these questions through a large part of the novel, artfully maintaining suspense by pausing from time to time to explore segments of another character's experience, an exercise in nonsequential narrative that helps to enhance the overall effect of spurious complication.

It turns out that Stingo's survival as a writer is for the time being assured by a most remarkable happenstance, one that must be the purest example of Southern gothic moonshine to appear in our literature since the fiction of Thomas Nelson Page. Stingo learns that he has come into a small inheritance left him by his grandmother whose father had received the money from the sale of a slave just before the Civil War. The legacy had for all those years been bricked-up in a cubbyhole in the basement of the family house in North Carolina until Stingo's father had discovered its whereabouts. Thus, Stingo is saved for literature by the miraculous intervention of an ancestral *deus ex machina* and is freed to devote his spare time to seeking a solution to his sexual dilemma.

This proves to be exceedingly difficult. He has encounters with two young women, Leslie and Mary Alice, and much later is able to get to bed with the novel's heroine, the beautiful Sophie. But before that happens he is very nearly driven mad by Leslie and Mary Alice. It seems that Leslie is exclusively lingually erotic and will permit only French-kissing, which she and Stingo indulge in hour after tongue-aching hour. Mary Alice will allow him to take no liberties with her person whatsoever but is quite willing to gratify him by hand, which she does in a pleasureless and perfunctory fashion. Although there is a certain dismal comedy in all this, just what it has to do with the central story of Sophie is never made clear, evidently because Styron does not know.

Sophie comes into Stingo's life after he moves into a room beneath hers in a Brooklyn boarding house. He is repeatedly awakened by the noise of savage copulation above him, and of course in his condition he becomes each time crazed with lust. Considerable suspense is developed over whether or not the ceiling will fall in on Stingo and just who the frenzied performers may be. Finally, he learns that they are Sophie, a Polish girl who has survived Auschwitz, and Nathan, a New York Jew who has nursed Sophie back to health after her ordeal and who claims to be a scientist. Stingo soon befriends the lovers and from then on becomes more and more deeply preoccupied with trying to penetrate the meaning of their strange contradictory relationship.

He is particularly mystified by the sudden and seemingly unprovoked shifts in Nathan's mood. He and Sophie will be making riotous love, and immediately afterward he will fall into a screaming rage, beat her bloody, and denounce her for having done something reprehensible in order to survive Auschwitz. This kind of behavior or some variation on it is repeated over and over again, to Stingo's steadily accelerating mystification, until at last Nathan's rage has been inflated into a force of seemingly cosmic vengeance and Sophie's guilty secret is made to seem as blackly criminal as the Holocaust itself. In fact, so much melodramatic voltage is generated not only by Nathan's violence and Stingo's anguish over it but by the soaring grandiloquence of Styron's prose that one might suppose the stage were being set for a performance of Götterdämmerung.

But it is through such pyrotechnics so carefully calculated to arouse expectations of the deepest tragedy and evil (What, in the name of Heaven, did Sophie DO?) that Styron attempts to justify devoting so much space to a detailed documentation of Sophie's life in Poland before the war; the happiness of her childhood; the unhappiness of her marriage; the arrest and execution of her father and her husband by the Nazis; the birth of her two children; the crime for which she was sent to Auschwitz (she had been caught smuggling a ham into Warsaw);

her experiences in the camp; her life in the household of the camp commandant; her relations with other inmates; the lesbian attacks made upon her by various women; her separation from her children and the presumed execution of her daughter; the Allied liberation of the camp. And throughout the narrative Styron is careful to drop periodic hints that if the reader will just stay with him a little longer, the unspeakable truth will come out.

But the fact is that Sophie's story is a windy record of Styron's apparent search for some way to legitimize the direful promises of his rhetoric, the extreme intensity of Nathan's wrath, the whole elaborate orchestration of Stingo's anguish and Sophie's ostensible damnation. For the truth about her supposed sin, when finally, *finally* it does emerge, represents not only a terrible anticlimax but an abdication of authorial responsibility, and the reader has every right to feel defrauded. If Sophie has sinned at all, her sin is at most venial and in the circumstances altogether understandable. Upon her arrival at Auschwitz she was forced by a drunken SS officer to decide whether her son or her daughter would be sent to the gas chamber. Sophie's choice was to save her son, but since she was *forced* to choose, the culpability belonged to the officer and not to her. Later, she had been able, because of her stenographic skills, to do clerical work for the camp commandant and so had escaped execution. She had also, in the hope of saving her son's life, offered herself to her employer, but he refused her. After he was transferred out of the camp, she suffered just as much as any of the other survivors.

Nathan really has no rational grounds for his suspicion of her and no justification for abusing her, particularly since Sophie has told him nothing about either her "choice" or her relations with the commandant. Furthermore, Nathan, after having been blown up by Styron into a kind of vengeful Old Testament Jehovah, is revealed to be nothing of the sort. He is, we discover, quite simply a paranoid schizophrenic and drug addict who has been lying about the important scientific work he is supposed to have been doing and whose goal is to persuade Sophie to join him in a suicide pact. Her second "choice" of death, therefore, seems not an act of atonement for a guilt which, after all, she lacks sufficient reason for having, but an indication that finally she is as insane as he is.

Thus, with Nathan's role and authority as a force of moral retribution invalidated by psychosis and Sophie's sin revealed to be petty, the novel is deprived of all ethical and thematic rationale, and its great length would seem to be a reflection of Styron's hope that if he described his characters and their actions through a sufficient quantity of pages he would sooner or later blunder on his theme.

Perhaps because of his Southern gothic heritage Styron has long had a hunger to engage the large seminal issues of good and evil, guilt, betrayal, revenge, and redemption. This is the message of his often quite eloquent prose: it aches for a subject portentous enough to justify its preacherly hellfire-and-brimstone tonalities. Styron needs, in fact, something of what the Puritan fathers, for all their fierce disdain for the secular life, possessed and we have lost: a coherent metaphysical view of the moral nature of existence. But all he has are urgent moral *sentiments* and quantities of raw material, which he is unable to make significant within an ideological context. The result is, as both this novel and *Set This House on Fire* make clear, that Styron is driven, in his effort to create the effect or illusion of significance, to resorting to all manner of sham theatrics and specious intimations that there exist large meanings just beneath the surface of his materials, that dark and inscrutable fates, dooms, and curses are hard at work shaping the grim destinies of his characters, even as they themselves repeatedly prove incapable of sustaining the great epic weight he tries to impose upon them.

Hence, instead of a situation of high tragedy, Styron is left in this novel with a kind of sad comedy. Instead of horrendous sin, he has in Sophie a pathetic case of self-preserving and quite justified expediency. Instead of sacred vengeance, he has in Nathan a case of profound mental disturbance. And in Stingo he clearly has a case of infinitely protracted adolescence. Like the characters in *Set This House on Fire* they are all too weakly human and spiritually impoverished to become principals in the great Sophoclean melodrama Styron tries so strenuously to hoke up for them. They are, in short, creatures of the contemporary moral void, while to serve Styron's purposes they need to be survivors of the great age of antiquity when the gods and goddesses laid down the laws and vented their terrible wrath on all transgressors.

Because he is deficient in a sense of what his materials are supposed to mean, Styron has a tendency to lapse into bathos and banality or weepy declarations of what Bellow once called "potato love" whenever he is required to express an attitude or make a generalization about the events that have occurred in his narrative. An excellent illustration is the closing scene of *Sophie's Choice* where we find Stingo, after having attended the funerals of Sophie and Nathan, lying on a beach in the middle of the night, grieving over his dead friends, and pondering the wisdom of the statement *"Let your love flow out on all living things."*

> It was then that the tears finally spilled forth . . . tears . . . I had tried manfully to resist and could resist no longer, having kept them so bottled up that now, almost alarmingly, they drained out in warm rivulets between my fingers. I did not weep for the six million Jews or the two million Poles or the one million Serbs or the five million Russians—I was unprepared to weep for all humanity—but I did weep for those others who in one way or another had become dear to me, and my sobs made an unashamed racket across the abandoned beach. Then I had no more tears to shed, and lowered myself to the sand on legs that suddenly seemed strangely frail and rickety for a man of twenty-two.
>
> When I awoke it was early morning. I lay looking straight up at the blue-green sky with its translucent shawl of mist; like a tiny orb of crystal, solitary and serene, Venus shone through the haze above the quiet ocean. I heard children chattering nearby. . . . Blessing my resurrection, I realized that the children had covered me with sand, protectively, and that I lay safe as a mummy beneath this fine, enveloping overcoat. It was then that in my mind I inscribed the words: *"Neath cold sand I dreamed of death/but woke at dawn to see/in glory, the bright, the morning star."*

Surely, there is a novel of the greatest tragic dimension to be written about the Holocaust. But just as surely, Styron has not written it, for with all its pretensions to literary majorness, *Sophie's Choice* is clearly a phony book, as imaginatively inauthentic as it is intellectually without content.

CHAPTER VII

The Troubles of Realism

Styron's failure to achieve a successful imaginative conception of the Holocaust may well be an example of the difficulty confronting contemporary novelists when, for reasons of talent and temperament, they are not content to create metaphors of nihilism and apocalypse, but wish rather to comment more or less directly and realistically on current social or political issues or to render as faithfully as possible the quality and character of the human condition in our time. The studies that follow have to do with four writers whose work might be considered to exemplify other aspects of this difficulty and some of the possible ways of overcoming it, achieving accommodation with it, or capitulating before it.

There is some firm evidence in the novels she has so far published that Alison Lurie should be a better novelist than she is. Her reputation up to now does not indicate that she has been widely appreciated for the qualities she does possess, although she has acquired over the years a certain small cult following, and her fifth novel, *The War Between the Tates*, which was made into a film, won her, however briefly, the kind of popular attention that may have proved only that her limitations had at last been recognized as seeming more attractive than her virtues. That novel, at any rate, represented a descent from some relatively serious level of intention into a flossiness that was only occasionally detectable in her before and which may well be attracting her natural public.

Yet from time to time even there and in the best of her earlier work Lurie reveals qualities that merit—and have seldom been given—close critical consideration. She has a satirical edge that, when it is not employed in hacking away at the obvious, is often eviscerating. She writes a prose of great clarity and precision, an expository language that efficiently serves her subject, but that does not stylize on it. She has many true things to say about the various modes of self-deception and distraction by which we endure the passage of life in these peculiarly trivializing times, and she often says them in a manner she has earned entirely by herself and that represents an authentic fictional voice. Yet there is also something hobbled and hamstrung about her engagement of experience, something that causes her again and again to fall short of what one feels to be her full capacity to extract the truth of her materials. She seems regularly to be aware of more than she can imaginatively comprehend, to be able to describe more than, like Styron, she can make thematically significant. Above all, there is a lack in her of the kind of adventurousness usually associated with important talent, a conventionality or timidity that frequently causes her to make formulations of reality that, in a part of her mind, she must know to be clichés and to pass over without examining certain possibilities for satire that a more radical talent would recognize as the most fertile possibilities to be found in her chosen subject.

These deficiencies manifest themselves perhaps most clearly in Lurie's heavy dependence on sexual intrigue for the dramatic complication of her fiction. In all her novels except *Imaginary Friends*, which seems to have no recognizable place in her canon, there is a monotonous sameness of situation that might appear to represent a ringing of changes on, and a progressively deepening exploration of an obsessive subject until one sees that really there is no changing or deepening. *Love and Friendship, The Nowhere City, Real People*, and *The War Between the Tates* all have to do with the experience of adultery, usually as enacted by academics or artists upon other academics and artists or by academics upon academic wives and graduate students. The setting in each case is the university community or artist colony —in *Real People* it is a barely disguised Yaddo—and as a rule the sexual drama is given such force as it possesses through being played out against the background of the dreariest middle-class respectability, boredom, child-breeding, and generalized spiritual and material shabbiness. What usually happens is that as a result of having good sex with somebody not one's legal spouse, the errant husband or wife achieves some temporary sense of rejuvenated identity that may or may not be to the ultimate advantage of marriage and community.

It is one of the older saws of criticism that extramarital sex in literature is not of terribly much interest in itself, however graphically it may be described. Its value lies in the illumination it gives to character and in the extent to which it poses some fresh challenge to the always fragile balance of tensions existing between the erotic imperatives of the self and the official hypocrisies of the public world. The penetration of the illusion that snobbery generates is, in Lionel Trilling's excellent phrase, the proper aim of the social novel, and adultery is one of the traditional, if hackneyed modes through which this aim is accomplished. But Lurie seems never to grasp the implications of the melodrama around which four of her five novels are constructed, and there are insufficient moral prohibitions in the society she describes to give it the depth of implication she is unable to perceive within it. She appears to feel that it is enough if her characters dare to commit the heresy of climbing into bed with one another. That is enough to ensure their meaning as characters and to justify their presence in her novels. Her treatment of adultery suffers, in short, from arbitrariness and inconsequence. The insight it affords us into the natures of the people who commit it is finally reducible to some idea of the beneficial or destructive effects of orgasmal liberation, which is repeatedly seen as in and for itself an apocalyptic experience. The academic husband in *The War Between the Tates* finds his graduate student a more imaginative and responsive lay than his timorous, rather frigid wife. The academic wife in *Love and Friendship* is sexually awakened by a professor of music, in *Nowhere City* by a California psychiatrist. As a result, the lives of these people either do or do not undergo some important change—a sufficiency of meaning perhaps in the one-dimensional world of the soap opera serial, where what happens next may finally be all that matters, but a gross insufficiency in novels that seem to promise some genuine revelation of character on a plane subtler and more complicated than that simply of the variety of sexual things one does to others or others do to one.

It may be just here that Lurie can be seen to share the dilemma of any satirical novelist of manners whose work must depend for its vitality in some direct way upon the vitality of the life he is attempting to satirize. The dilemma is deepened, furthermore, when the novelist's subject is contemporary academic manners, for nothing is more obvious to anyone familiar with the university scene of the last twenty years than that the dramatic possibilities for a fiction dealing with academic life are not what they once were—nor has the gradual growth of an encrustation of cliché around some of its most typifying characters and situations made the problem any less difficult. It seems scarcely conceivable that a novelist of whatever degree of talent would be able to write academic fiction today without being obliged to write *through* the precedent established by such classic practitioners of the genre as Helen Howe, Mary McCarthy, Randall Jarrell, Robie Macauley, and Bernard Malamud, at the same time that he would necessarily be writing without most of the advantages these writers possessed.

If it is true that effective satire depends on the disparity between pretense and practice, self-delusion and the reality that reveals it to be in fact self-delusion, then it is clear that these essential elements, while they obviously continue to exist in academic life, no longer exist in conditions that once caused them to seem representative of that life, nor are they embodied in personality types that once made them easily accessible to the satirist. The pompous and priggish or bumbling and generally ineffectual professor was a reality in American universities long before he became the paradigmatic buffoon figure in a hundred academic novels—and so too was the lecherous or the politically vicious professor through whom it was possible to dramatize the comic contrast between the principles of monastic dedication and intellectual disinterestedness normally attributed to the teaching profession and the prurience and petty-mindedness so often visible behind the pious façade. It is very much the sort of contrast so effectively dramatized in *M*A*S*H*, the popular television series about a medical team assigned to a field hospital during the Korean War. Just as the academic novel typically exploits our expectation that professors are, or ought to be Olympian, the series exploits our assumption that practitioners of medicine are at all times noble and heroic. The spectacle of doctors swapping cynical jokes while probing a battle casualty's viscera for shell fragments outrages our pieties and makes us laugh, not merely at the incongruity of the conduct, but at the pieties that have caused us to see the conduct as incongruous. And so, for similar reasons, we might laugh at the spectacle of academics sabotaging their colleagues in the committee room or copulating with their students on the committee room floor.

But all this is dependent upon traditional patterns of moral expectation and idealization inherited from the past and made habitual to us through our exposure to them in past literature, and they are coming to have less and less relation to the actualities of either the medical or the academic profession. In fact, most of the qualities we have traditionally attributed to occupational groups—primness in female schoolteachers, sanctimoniousness in clergymen, obsequiousness in salespeople, competitiveness in businessmen—no longer accurately characterize these groups and are therefore no longer valid as attributions when used for the purposes of satire. What obviously has happened is that all those groups have come increasingly to resemble one another in their styles of behavior and personality. The new egalitarianism, which is a matter of both political and psychological orientation, has homogenized their characteristics, washed out such idiosyncrasies as they may once have possessed, and made it extremely difficult to distinguish among them. In academic life this has become particularly evident and is perhaps more striking than elsewhere, if only because the teaching profession, like the medical, has been among the most heavily burdened by moral idealizations projected by those who still take seriously the moral valuation academics once placed upon themselves. Hence, it is possible for large numbers of otherwise enlightened people to read novels featuring characters modeled on professors *as they used to be* and feel satisfied that they have been given a realistic view of academic life as it now is. Yet the truth is that over the last twenty years the realities of academic life have drastically changed. Through a process of perhaps inevitable attrition, coupled with the damage done by the student activist movement of the sixties, the self-esteem of professors has been eroded to the point where it is now a better subject for pathos than for satire. The typifying academic stance today is not self-importance, but self-deprecation, not the severity that accompanies the effort to enforce intellectual standards, but the laxity that follows from the loss of a sense of standards and a fear that if standards in fact do continue to exist, it would in some way be dangerous or undemocratic to enforce them. Particularly among younger faculty members it is possible to identify a new personality style characterized by a nervous, ingratiating geniality, a seemingly cultivated limpness of manner, a carelessness of speech and dress, an air of humility and apology, that inside or outside the classroom might identify them with equal justice as Madison Avenue junior executives, junior State Department officials, or, for that matter, junior shoe clerks. Their pretension is, if anything, their complete lack of pretension. Their self-delusion derives not from a belief that they are consecrated to a special calling and are therefore above the temptations that beset ordinary men, but rather that they are no different from anybody else, have no wish to be, and would be perfectly satisfied if they could be left alone to pursue the modest pleasures of being ordinary. Unfortunately for the satirist, this sense of ordinariness is, in the case of a great many academics, not in the least self-delusory but issues from an altogether sound assessment of the facts. Hence, there is no snobbery to be penetrated, no pomposity for the satirist to deflate.

Another feature of academic life made obsolete by the devolutionary processes of history is the experience, which until fairly recently most professors could take for granted, of inhabiting in the university a social organism that is parochial, intimate, restrictive, and closely monitory. Academic novelists of the past found their most dependable source of dramatic tension in the conflict between individual characters and the pressures of a society in which they felt confined or too much under scrutiny, so that if they misbehaved, they risked exposure, scandal, even the possibility of professional disaster. Such a society may still exist in some of the smaller academic communities, but it is no longer typical of the academic experience in general. What is much more common today is the abstracted and depersonalized situation of the multiversity, and it is extremely difficult to see how the kind of intrigue that interests Lurie and has interested other novelists before her could have very much meaning or reality there. The members of a multiversity society are usually notable for the hypothetical nature of their sense of belonging to a society and by their merely propinquitous connection with one another. Human relations are tenuous at best or exclusively professional at worst, and it is entirely possible to exist for years in the multiversity complex without knowing or particularly caring to know what one's colleagues are doing in their extra-curricular lives. There would, furthermore, be very little likelihood that they would be capable of committing any act heinous enough to bring down upon them collective censure or even collective notice, not only because academics are remarkable for their lack of daring, but also because the social and moral terms by which the conduct of others can be related significantly to oneself or judged in relation to the community have either broken down or never existed.

What one is finally forced to confront is the progressive trivialization of academic life in America, a process surely connected with the erosion of professorial self-esteem and the loss of a sense of existing among human realities in a real society. But the serious consequence not only for those who care personally about the quality of academic life but for a novelist committed, as Lurie seems to be, to making literary use of that life is quite simply a diminishment of dramatic possibility, the decline of specific experiences involving contingency and risk, the threat of exposure and the sacrifice of something precious, important, or necessary. Professors can scarcely be ridiculed by the satirist for sabotaging one another in the committee room if they assume that in so doing they are merely playing the customary dirty politics of academic life. There is very little drama left in student-faculty love affairs if they no longer carry the potential of having dire consequences. In these days they can so easily pass undetected; the girl can get through the course with high marks and unpregnant; the professor can keep the girl and his tenure.

In Lurie's fiction of academic life a situation that may once have been crucial may seem to be of uncertain significance or to have a merely hoked-up significance just because the actualities of academic life have depleted it of drama. The student in *The War Between the Tates* will either marry the professor or she will not. If she gets pregnant, as she finally does, she will either have an abortion or she will run off, as she finally does, with an accommodating young man to a commune in California where she will give birth to what may or may not be the professor's child. Before the descent of this *deus ex machina*, the professor's wife has already seriously considered giving him a divorce so that he will be free to marry the girl. But since the girl decides to leave, that measure proves unnecessary, and at the end of the novel it appears that the professor either will or will not return to his wife. On the face of it, such problems would seem to be swollen with dramatic, not to say melodramatic possibility. But they actually are not because we recognize that behind them there is absolutely nothing at stake—no risk, no threat, no anguish. The society in which they and the characters exist is much too limited, drab, and morally diffuse to give them consequence. In fact, the defining feature of that society is its power to draw all potential extremes of conduct into a dead middle, a deactivating nullity, to see to it that actions shall *have* no consequences, that nobody will have to suffer or pay or be put to any kind of serious inconvenience. It is a society made for and by the burgeoning new population of academic Babbitts, and it is the ideal medium for their relentlessly bourgeois pursuits, their child-breeding, their house- and car-pride, their little gourmet dinners, the undisturbed cultivation of their ordinariness.

There is evidence in Lurie's novels that she has some awareness of this aspect of academic life, but she treats it as little more than stage-setting for her favorite drama of sexual intrigue. Perhaps it would require a talent the size of Mailer's or Bellow's to recognize that just here, in the contrast between the professional function of academics and their way of life, is to be found what little remains of interesting literary material in the university scene. These supposedly gifted and fearless seekers after truth, these staunch defenders of the things of the mind and the spirit, the best that has been thought and said, living out their days in complacent scruffiness—the incongruity is both ludicrous and rather frightening, and it could form the basis of a great subject. But Lurie's novels do not engage it because her imagination remains trapped amid the clichés of academic life, in situations history has rendered obsolete and in crises that have lost their power, in both actuality and art, to matter very much.

Conceivably, it may now be possible for a white critic to judge James Baldwin on his merits as a novelist without inciting all the liberal pieties to riot, and without at the same time minimizing the importance of the very great deal he has taught us about the black experience in America. Over the past thirty years Baldwin has become the most influential prophet and polemicist and perhaps the most distinguished writer of his race, and he has earned a position in the moral community of our time comparable only to that of Norman Mailer as a monitor of conscience and a remaker of consciousness. With his fame now secure, we have accorded him the highest honor we can bestow upon a public intellectual: we have disarmed him with celebrity, fallen in love with his eccentricities, and institutionalized his outrage, along with Mailer's obscenity and Capote's bitchiness, into prime-time entertainment.

Yet his role as America's favorite token black is not without its advantages for Baldwin the writer, however responsible it may have been for converting the realities of his cause into the clichés of rhetoric. His strategy has always been to keep constantly before us the reminder that he is a *black* writer and that black is his subject. The absolute rightness of his cause coupled with his self-righteousness in proselytizing for it have very effectively kept at bay many commentators who might otherwise have approached him with the critical skepticism they habitually bring to the work of his white contemporaries. Baldwin has, to be sure, been the object of negative criticism, but all too often its force has been blunted or misdirected to peripheral issues, seemingly in deference to the idea that the act of critical discrimination just might possibly be considered discriminatory. Where other writers may be judged on the strength of their artistry, Baldwin's artistry has frequently been placed beyond judgment because of the sacredness of his subject. One can only wonder whether his other and, in some respects, more central subject, interracial sexuality and homosexuality, would be quite so effective as a silencer of opposition.

But the serious problem for any minority writer—whether black, Jewish, Catholic, Irish, or Iroquois—is that he is so seldom able to transcend the limits of the minority experience. Since his psyche has to some degree been traumatized by it, his imaginative vision can become petrified within it. Writers who are socially identified only to the extent that they are German or British or Wasp American have no such difficulty, and very often as a result they are hard put to discover a subject. Baldwin's blackness has caused him to perceive and conceive experience almost exclusively within the charged polarities of black and white, and in spite of his intelligence and remarkable powers of narration—qualities displayed more impressively in his essays than in his novels—he has repeatedly produced fictional characterizations that represent the most simplistic vision of the racial conflict. There is considerable irony in this because Baldwin, very early in his career, brilliantly stated the case against the very kind of fiction he later came to write. In the well-known essay, "Everybody's Protest Novel," composed during the writing of his own first novel, *Go Tell It on the Mountain*, he attacked *Uncle Tom's Cabin* on the ground of its sentimentality and the stereotypical nature of its characters and then went on to warn of the dangers inherent for the novelist in a mechanical and collectivist view of human beings, the subordination of the individual in his complexity and unpredictability to the service of some socio-political issue or cause. "The failure of the protest novel lies," he said, "in its rejection of life, the human being, the denial of his beauty, dread, power, in its insistence that it is his categorization alone which is real and which cannot be transcended." However sensitive Baldwin may be to the unique quality of the individual human being, he has been generally unsuccessful in creating characters who exist independently of their categorization. He has also been guilty, particularly in his later fiction, of the "self-righteous, virtuous sentimentality, the ostentatious parading of excessive and spurious emotion" of which he accuses Harriet Beecher Stowe. Baldwin attributes this failing to an "inability to feel." In his own case, it would appear to be the result of an inability to extricate his undoubtedly powerful feelings for individual people from his far more powerful feelings for them as victims of racial oppression.

Perhaps in an effort to break out of the confines and generalize the implications of his own form of the protest novel, Baldwin has repeatedly tried to convince his readers that there is finally no difference between the dilemma of his black characters and that of just about everybody else in our corrupt society. To be black in America seems to him the same thing as to be American. John Grimes, the protagonist of *Go Tell It on the Mountain*, could be any sensitive boy of any color who happens to be in conflict with his environment. To be an American black in Harlem or Atlanta is no different from being an American black in Paris, where a black may, as Baldwin has said, discover himself to be "as American as any Texas G.I." Furthermore, to be a white homosexual in America is to be as oppressed and fugitive as any black; indeed, to be an American at all seems tantamount, in Baldwin's view, to being in some sense sexually ambivalent. Deep down beneath the layers of color and nationality we are all brothers and we are all queer.

Whatever small truth there may be in such majestic conjunctions would appear to be outweighed by the fact of Baldwin's own anguish over the *special* predicament of blacks in this country, to say nothing of the abundant evidence of the realities of that predicament to be found in his essays and novels. If the black problem is everybody's problem, then it is clearly fallacious to isolate it as a black problem and to view it with such extreme indignation.

Baldwin's preoccupation with sexual love between blacks and whites may be yet another symptom of his effort to extend the thematic range of his fiction beyond the boundaries of race. Sexual love emerges in his novels as a kind of universal anodyne for the disease of racial separatism, as a means not only of achieving personal identity but of transcending false categories of color and gender. It may not be excessive to claim, as Marcus Klein has done, that love represents for Baldwin "the perfect democracy, the new Eden, wherein all complicating distinctions since Eden will have disappeared." There is, in fact, a sustained dramatic contrast throughout his fiction between the generalized tensions of prejudice and hostility, as they exist in the public environment of the action, and the intimacy and trust existing between the friends and lovers who make up the inner community of principal characters. As the forces of discrimination grow stronger in the outside world, the characters grow more undiscriminating in their sexuality, achieving through countless combinations and recombinations of relationship some brief sense that they are still alive. In *Another Country*, the most sexually strenuous of Baldwin's novels, there are affairs between a black male musician and a Southern white woman, a white male homosexual actor and a white housewife, a black woman and a white male heterosexual writer, who spends one night of love with the actor, who in his turn once had an affair with the musician.

The remarkable thing about these people, apart from their indefatigability, is that they are really not interested in one another at all. In fact, they are no more real to one another than they are as characters. They do not share common tastes, interests, or ideas, only bed, and when they are out of bed, which is seldom, they talk endlessly about trivia, consume great quantities of food, cigarettes, and liquor, and moon about feeling vast unutterable emotions of tenderness and loyalty. Very little happens in *Another Country* except copulation and conversation. Yet Baldwin obviously takes it all very seriously. He wraps his characters round and round with skeins of "self-righteous and virtuous sentimentality" and describes them in precisely the rhetoric of "excessive and spurious emotion" he found so distasteful in *Uncle Tom's Cabin*. One might have assumed on the evidence of his essays and early fiction that

Baldwin would be consumed in the fires of hate and that his future as a novelist could well depend on his attainment of compassion and objectivity. But it seemed probable after the appearance of *Another Country* and the later novel, *Tell Me How Long the Train's Been Gone*, that he might instead be destined to drown in the throbbing seas of sentimental love, and, regrettably, his next novel, *If Beale Street Could Talk*, only served to make that probability seem an absolute certainty.

The atmosphere of that novel was so pretentious and cloying with good will and loving kindness and humble fortitude and generalized honorableness that one had to think back to Saroyan's Armenians and Steinbeck's Tortilla Flat charmers to find an adequate comparison. Clearly, the novelist of protest carries somewhere within his soul a vision of the kind of Utopia that might emerge if only the conditions he is protesting against were corrected and those who now hate one another could be persuaded to see just how lovable their enemies really are. In his previous two novels Baldwin produced fantasies of black-white relationships in which various characters loved and lusted after one another seemingly *just because* they belonged to different races. In the process, he took very large liberties with the truth about such relationships as they normally exist in our society and, by so doing, may unwittingly have confirmed an impression certain whites would be eager to embrace: there actually is no race problem in America that cannot be solved by the application of a little tenderness and the recognition that what we all really want is to enjoy splendid sex together.

In *If Beale Street Could Talk* Baldwin produced yet another fantasy of rather larger social implications, this time one in which the characters of black people living in contemporary Harlem are shown to be so noble and courageous that one is constrained to wonder how we ever imagined that conditions in the black urban ghettoes are anything other than idyllic. If to be black is to be beautiful, to be poor and black is to be positively saintly. Yet another fiction of great attractiveness to the white mind is thus perpetrated: ghetto blacks are really very happy with their lot. In fact, they are just as simple and fun-loving and warm-hearted as the grinning old darkies of Southern song and legend.

To be sure, there is a good deal of adversity in *If Beale Street Could Talk,* but it is there just to demonstrate how well the characters can cope with it and come through with courage undaunted and tempers unsullied. A nineteen-year-old black girl named Tish is in love with and becomes pregnant by a young black sculptor named Fonny. They plan to be married, but Fonny is unjustly accused of raping a Puerto Rican woman and is sent to prison. The action turns on the efforts of Tish and her family to track down and persuade the woman that she has made a mistake and thus exonerate Fonny. For a variety of reasons this seems, by the close of the novel, a most unlikely possibility. The woman has disappeared into Puerto Rico. Fonny's trial has been indefinitely postponed and he remains in prison. Tish at the end is in process of giving birth. Amidst all these dark troubles, life is renewed and faith in life reaffirmed. Fonny, the sculptor, sits in prison "working on the wood, on the stone, whistling, smiling. And from far away, but coming nearer, the baby cries and cries and cries and cries and cries and cries and cries and cries, cries like it means to wake the dead." Thus, the novel's concluding lines.

It is extremely sad to see a writer of Baldwin's gifts producing, in all seriousness, such junk. Yet it has been evident for some time that he is deteriorating as a novelist and becoming increasingly a victim of the vice of sentimentality. This seems a particular pity because Baldwin may have one important novel left within him which it would take the most radical courage to write, the story of a talented black writer who achieves worldwide success on the strength of his anger and, in succeeding, gradually loses his anger and comes to be loved by everyone. Clearly, such acceptance can be considered a triumph for a black man in America, but it can be death for a black writer in whom anger and talent are indivisible.

There now seems to be widespread agreement—not only among his literary contemporaries but large segments of the reading public—that, in spite of close competition from Saul Bellow, Norman Mailer remains the most vital and important writer we have today. The interesting question is why this presumably self-evident fact of Mailer's large stature has taken so long to be acknowledged, why even sophisticated people have had to *learn* to live with it as if it were a loathsome disease, after overcoming extremely powerful feelings of distaste, while legions of the semiliterate, the sort who never read books but know exactly which writers they detest, appear to harbor the most astonishing hostility to Mailer's face, physique, voice, manners, and morals and seem unable to understand why he was not put away long ago.

This is rather odd when one considers that we have never expected our best writers to be particularly saintly and that there is a fine tradition among them of behavior ranging from the merely perverse through the boorish, sottish, deceitful, spiteful, disloyal, and infantile to the maddest reaches of paranoia and monomania. The examples of Poe, Whitman, Twain, Frost, Hart Crane, Hemingway, Faulkner, and Fitzgerald all testify in varying degrees to the fact that sometimes the only respectable thing about a writer is his writing. Yet these men have been accepted—in some cases, to be sure, only after they were decorously dead—because the quality of their work finally seemed to justify their peculiarities of character.

The trouble with Mailer is that not only has he been very much alive among us—unforgivably alive—but he seemed for too long a dubious quantity as a writer, while his character grew steadily more outrageous. There was a period in the fifties when he appeared to imagine that the way to achieve large literary success was to engage in brawls and try to get arrested or to insult his readers by disparaging their intelligence—as he did to such good effect in the columns he wrote at the time for *The Village Voice.* His strategy then may well have been to create such an offensive public image that people would be moved to read him if only out of hate. But the practical result was that too many people decided that nobody who acted that foolish could possibly be worth reading. Significantly, it was not until the appearance, in 1959, of *Advertisements for Myself,* a collection offered quite nakedly, even abjectly, as an appeal for serious recognition, that the tide of opinion began to turn in Mailer's favor, and it did so not because that book contained old material hitherto unappreciated or prompted a reconsideration of his novels, but because in writing about his frustrations and mistakes, the wreck of his literary hopes, the corrosions of failure that drove him to behave badly, he produced a prose so remarkably better than anything he had done before that a large number of readers saw for the first time how very good a writer he was—because then, for the first time, he was that good.

Mailer also discovered in *Advertisements* what has since become his most complex and vital subject—himself as combined victim, adversary, hero, and fool being simultaneously humiliated and aggrandized as he engages the ogres and windmills of contemporary history. He had learned a great deal about the dramatic possibilities inherent in the multifoliate subject of Norman Mailer, and he was destined as time passed to learn a great deal more. But by 1959 his remarkable sensitivity to the intricate telegraphies of status had already taught him this much: that to be taken seriously as a man and writer you do not *demand* the approval of the public, for this puts you in the position of appearing to feel arrogantly superior to them and insisting on what is rightfully your due. The far better way is to make the public feel superior to you by demonstrating how pathetic you have become in trying to win their approval and just how much their approval means to you. Furthermore, you could always count on good Americans to believe that recognition should come to those who have worked for it hard enough, and Mailer in *Advertisements* had explained with fine eloquence how terribly hard he had worked for it. If, as Leslie Fiedler once remarked, nothing succeeds for Americans like failure, it is equally true that confession of failure is not only cleansing to the soul but absolutely wonderful for one's public image.

Having apparently learned all this by 1959, Mailer went on to learn something even more essential to his future prosperity: how to make himself into the kind of writer who would finally neutralize through his work some of the mistrust and hostility he had generated through his public behavior. He achieved this in two ways. First, he began making much more direct use in his fiction of his own well-publicized obsessions and aberrations—his interest in the mystical properties of the orgasm in *The Time of Her Time*, the spiritually regenerative effects of wife-murder in *An American Dream*, the cathartic possibilities of the scatalogical in *Why Are We in Vietnam?*. This had the effect of dissociating these ideas from his public self and the essays and interviews in which he had first presented them as shockingly offensive personal interests, and giving them the safely general and objective quality of fictional themes. As such, they might still seem offensive, but at least they would be identified with his imaginary characters and no longer be taken as quite such literal evidence of his own moral corruption.

At the same time he was also discovering how to project in his work—primarily in the meta-journalism he began to write in the late sixties—a self-image that became steadily more attractive, not so much because the things he described himself as saying and doing had suddenly ceased to seem outrageous, but because a new note of humor had come to characterize the description and to give it an air of ironic detachment and ambiguity that was both appealing and enormously effective as a tranquilizer of enemies. He was no longer the victim of his buldgeoning first-person delivery. Instead, Mailer became his own most derisive critic as he observed his various personae—an aging, hungover activist in Washington, "the reporter" in Miami and Chicago, Aquarius in Cape Kennedy and Houston—pass through the postures of acute embarrassment, ineptitude, braggadocio, affectation, and occasional wisdom, hamming it up for the gallery or putting down a rival, but always finally being put down hardest by himself. The traits displayed by these personae had long been fixtures of Mailer's public character, but when he had displayed them in that character they had earned him little more than hostility. Now the writer in him had found a way of using them as material, and in the process he turned his worst vices into almost lovable virtues. The early Mailer committed the one sin Americans never forgive: he took himself seriously. As a journalist, he began to laugh at himself—an action we prize even more highly than failure.

In achieving these realignments Mailer can hardly be accused of cynicism. There is nothing to indicate that he was employing his skills as a politician, although they are recognized to be considerable. He seems rather to have passed into a new phase of personal and creative development in which he was able to engage himself and his material in fresh terms. By the late sixties he had gained in wisdom as well as age, and he had also gained sufficient success to appease at least the larger hungers of his ego and give him a certain benevolent detachment. But that these things occurred at this particular time was highly fortunate, and so was the fact that he began just then to offer in his journalism a kind of material singularly appropriate to the historical moment and guaranteed to have a major impact particularly on the younger audience of the moment.

It had been obvious for years to others, if not to Mailer, that if he expected, as he claimed, to have a revolutionary influence on the consciousness of the age, he would be unlikely to do so through the novel. The problem was not simply that his best talents were only erratically displayed in the novel, but that the form itself seemed inadequate to satisfy the needs of a generation who had grown to believe that the social realities of this world are far more important than imaginative fictions, and who were trying to relate to issues as the generation before them had tried to relate to ideas. Mailer's interests as a writer and those of his largest potential public thus nicely coincided, for it had been evident—perhaps even as far back as *The Naked and the Dead* —that his particular powers found their most intense stimulus in moments of social and political crisis, in apocalyptic confrontations between individuals and the massive forces of historical and institutional change. The march on the Pentagon, the riots in Chicago, the Presidential conventions of 1968 were all charged with apocalyptic portent. They were as beautifully suited to Mailer's temperament and style as if he had invented them himself—which, in fact, he might have done—and it so happened that all the seismic instruments agreed that these occasions demanded expression in precisely the form he and he alone could give them.

If he had come to envision himself as a symptomatic consciousness mediating between his personal micro-hells and the major disasters of his age, he now had an audience desperately in need of someone on whom they could project their own more incoherent sense of being both agents and dupes of history, at once personally implicated in and collectively victimized by events. What they found in Mailer was a writer who could bring into focus the contradictory elements of this feeling, a spokesman able to express it in language and action more forcefully than they could or would have dared and, above all, a human being whom they could accept—as they had accepted no one since John Kennedy—as a hero because he epitomized in his humanness the ambiguities necessary to an acceptable heroism at that time. He was tough, brash, defiantly irreverent, a taker of unbelievable risks. But he was also—and openly admitted to being—vulnerable, uncertain, fearful of the impression he was making (on Robert Lowell, Dwight Macdonald, Eugene McCarthy, Sonny Liston), never completely convinced of the possibility that mere quaking guts might stand up to their monolithic self-possession.

Yet that exactly was the secret of Mailer's appeal, the very essence of his heroism, for he was guts at war with all his unmastered contradictions and fears, and he monitored them in battle with that deadly obsessiveness of the general who has never quite grown up to the courage of his command, brooding over the corpses of real men when he should have been figuring the cold statistics of killed and wounded. Such men as Lowell, Liston, and McCarthy might be great poets, fighters, and politicians, but they could not be heroes, at least not in this time and generation, because they were too complete as personages, at once too intact in their fortitude and too remote from their mortality. Mailer was like the early characters of Hemingway, and of course he would like to have thought that he was more than a little like Hemingway himself. He was all blustering defense mechanism, the hairy fist clutching the fragile rose, bravery earned at the expense of panic, a mass of insecurities constantly in need of the challenge that would force him into at least the appearance of strength. He thus dramatized the antithetical impulses that underlay the protest movement and the psychology of the young. He expressed their strong mistrust

of the pieties of the establishment at the same time that he
forced them to confront their own even more pompous pieties.
He embodied their sense of self-importance and of insignificance,
their faith and their cynicism, their desire to make the grand
gesture, and their intuition that the grand gesture would probably have slight effect on anyone, least of all the blind course of
history. Mailer, in short, was the perfect absurd white knight of
their mighty, absurd crusade—the quixotic figure of fun, nobility,
pride, self-derisiveness, and absolute honesty for a generation
that had nothing to offer but its indignation, its idealism, and its
preposterous nerve.

But one saw that these same qualities that made Mailer so
attractive to the younger readers of his journalism also helped
to ingratiate him with older readers and even former enemies.
That developing note of self-derisiveness that came to characterize
his treatment of his various personae was accompanied by an
increasing tendency to equivocate about issues and people he at
one time most probably would have demolished. Practically every
portrait he drew of public events and personalities could be seen
to have a dimension of meliorating ambiguity. If he put down
liberals, one also noticed that he put down conservatives. He
might show irritation over the fact that Ralph Abernathy had
kept the press waiting forty minutes in Miami. He might even
use the occasion to deliver one of his most agonized and eloquent
perorations on the whole oppressive phenomenon of Negro
rights:

> . . . he [Mailer] was so heartily sick of listening to the
> tyranny of soul music, so bored with Negroes triumphantly
> late for appointments, so depressed with Black inhumanity
> to Black in Biafra, so weary of being sounded in the subway
> by Black eyes, so despairing of the smell of booze and pot
> and used-up hope in the blood-shot eyes of Negroes bombed
> at noon. . . .

He might even acknowledge the presence in "some secret part
of his flesh (of) a closet Republican," yet the confession clearly
costs him something in "dread and woe." Its impact is softened
if not canceled by his so evident guilt, and that, it turns out, is

not his loss but his gain, for he has registered his heresy in the
very breath of denouncing it, and so may be said to have had it
both ways—to have put into words our most vicious buried
hatreds, but purged himself and us with the detergents of self-
disgust.

In the same manner one also saw him in *Armies of the Night*
open an attack on his peers, yet with a sure instinct for the right
one to destroy—Paul Goodman, lost to him anyway, but not
Lowell, or Macdonald, who at that moment was known to be
at work on a review of *Why Are We in Vietnam?* for *The New
Yorker*. Again, it would be unfair to suggest that what has really
happened to Mailer is that he has become a politician. Without
doubt his vision has simply grown more dialectical, and he has
found a way of dramatizing more completely his own intellectual
and psychological contradictions. Nevertheless, one cannot deny
that this often *appears* to be circumspection or that, deliberate
or not, it has worked powerfully to his advantage. He now
knows how little real profit there is in the self-indulgence of the
direct attack, and how much potential risk. To allow oneself
the exhilaration of trying with a single blow to kill off all one's
literary competitors—as he very nearly succeeded in doing in
"The Talent in the Room" and "Some Children of the Goddess"
—is to take the chance of undermining one's whole campaign
for the championship. Mailer did not dare to afford such luxuries
now that he saw he had become the caretaker of a possibly major
reputation and a talent for winning the large-scale approval he
had fought for throughout his literary life.

The dangers for the public writer in achieving approval of this
kind were all rehearsed for us in the sad example of Hemingway.
Mailer began by envying Hemingway his reputation and, now
that he has won something approaching its equivalent, there is
always the risk that he might be forced to suffer very similar
consequences. If Hemingway finally found it more enjoyable to
play at being the celebrity than to persist in the more arduous
course of developing himself as a writer, Mailer may not be
wholly exempt from the same temptation. Widespread attention
is most easily won these days through performing in the mass
media, and such performance is far less tiring than creativity.

If in order to gain an audience for your important work, you make yourself into a media performer, you must also know when to stop performing and get on with your important work. Otherwise, you may end by becoming nothing but a performer and, worse, you will begin to live for it as an end in itself. Mailer knows this better than most because he knows his own weaknesses better than anybody else, and the knowledge will undoubtedly save him. But now that he has proved that he can survive and triumph over failure, he has still to prove that he can survive his large success. To do this it would seem that he must learn again the lesson every successful artist has had to learn not once but many times: that it is necessary for him to become private once more because his real demons can never be confronted in the public limelight but only in the haunted personal dark. Yeats's lines addressed "To a Friend Whose Work Has Come to Nothing" may be even more appropriate to one whose work has come to a very great deal:

> Bred to a harder thing
> Than Triumph, turn away
> And like a laughing string
> Whereon mad fingers play
> Amid a place of stone,
> Be secret and exult,
> Because of all things known
> That is most difficult.

In choosing to describe *The Executioner's Song* as a "True Life Novel," Mailer has, with his accustomed audacity, shaken whatever may have been left of our confidence in the old standards by which it once seemed possible to distinguish between fact and fiction. If Mailer's account of the actual events and relationships of Gary Gilmore's last nine months of life can in any valid sense be called a novel, then clearly some drastic dislocation of categories has occurred. Fiction and fact have in some mysterious way changed places or have become so intertwined in recent years that they now, for all practical purposes, constitute a new literary form combining features that once enabled us to tell them apart.

The rise of the so-called New Journalism over the last two decades would seem to indicate that this kind of blending of genres has in fact occurred, and Mailer of course has contributed importantly to it. But Truman Capote, Tom Wolfe, Hunter S. Thompson, and others have also during that period produced books that treat actual persons and events from a personal perspective and in a variety of styles normally associated with fiction. At the same time such ostensible novelists as Heller in *Good as Gold*, E. L. Doctorow in *Ragtime*, and Kurt Vonnegut in *Jailbird* have combined their purely fictional characters with living or historical personages like Henry Kissinger, Richard Nixon, Roy Cohn, Emma Goldman, and Harry Houdini. We might well ask on what grounds such cohabitations and adulterations can be justified.

One perhaps obvious answer is that a substantial shift has taken place in our relation to and way of apprehending experience, a shift that has caused the old distinctions between the actual and the imaginary to become obsolete, and the new eclecticism of our prose literature represents a necessary and inevitable adjustment to the change. As the major events of our recent national history have more than adequately proven, our writers have been confronted with increasingly preposterous and stupifying assaults on their sense of credibility, and their power to imagine experience has, to paraphrase Philip Roth, been steadily outdone by actual happenings that seem completely unimaginable. What novelist could have invented the madness of the Kennedy assassinations or the Manson murders or the Jonestown suicides or Richard Nixon and Watergate or Jimmy Carter and brother Billy?

The point of course is that no novelist has needed to invent them. Such events represent the climactic dramas of our time, and the people involved in them are the protagonists and bit-players, heroes and anti-heroes—transported by the instantly publicizing powers of the mass media out of their real-life identities and fictionalized into beings more remarkable than any imaginable characters in fiction. With the help of the media, real life, in its consummate unreality, has, in short, usurped the role of the creative imagination and turned the news of the day into a novel, but without being able to do with it what a novelist would do—that is, give it the coloration and meaning of felt personal experience rather than the abstract and impersonal character of reported events occurring among strangers out there in the electronic void. If a writer is interested in trying to confront and make sense of these events, then he is obviously obliged to find some means of performing that task. He must restore them to the status of experiences that actually happened or might happen to someone. He must particularize, personalize, and humanize materials that, however bizarre they may be in their unreality, must be made to take on the reality required to give them meaning.

Some of our writers have tried to do this in differing ways. Capote in *In Cold Blood* was able to make at least in some degree understandable one of the most brutal and seemingly senseless of crimes by analyzing and humanizing the murderers and their victims in the manner of a novelist. As I have said, Mailer in *The Armies of the Night* appointed himself the chief character in the drama of the Pentagon march and so brought coherence and his special idiosyncratic moral perspective to that tumultuous mass action. In *The Executioner's Song* he does the exact opposite, keeping himself rigorously aloof from his narrative scene and viewing Gilmore and the people involved with him as characters who are creating their own novel out of what they are and do in real life. Mailer wisely allows them to speak for themselves in a variety of prose styles that mimic the manner in which they customarily think and speak, so that they are individualized by the distinctive personalities of their idioms at the same time that they are given dramatic coherence by the tightly choreographed nature of the case itself as it evolves from the murders Gilmore committed, through his trial and the efforts made to prevent his execution, to his death by firing squad. All Mailer had to do was keep himself out of his story and present actualities that were more compelling than anything he might have been able to imagine. As he said in an interview following the publication of the book, "What I had was gold, if I had enough sense not to gild it."

Other writers such as Pynchon, Hawkes, and Barth have

developed in a very different direction—away from the fictional treatment of actual events toward the creation of metaphorical and fabulative impressions of the kind of derangement that may be responsible for these events. Their characters and situations derive their validity not from their realistic resemblance to the actual, but rather from their emblematic relation to current conditions of moral breakdown, dehumanization, and social entropy. The often quite complex systems of meaning they create are internal to the particular work—for example, the rigid pattern of Herbert Stencil's obsessive pursuit of the mysterious V. has meaning only in contrast to the patternlessness of Benny Profane's relation to life. Yet as emblematic constructions they may have a significance in relation to the external world of the most profound kind.

These writers, furthermore, are highly aware—and evidently want their readers to be aware—that their works are fictions and that fictions can be as outlandish and baffling as anything that happens in real life. This may be their way of asserting that, in the midst of the prevailing unreality, the only thing we can be confident is real is the author's power of contrivance. Or if the distinctions between fact and fiction are fast disappearing, they may be emphasizing the artificiality of their fiction in the hope of preserving it from further contamination by the pollutants of fact. In this endeavor what Henry James called "the madness of art" may still have a chance of winning a modest victory over the encroaching madness of life.

Saul Bellow has all along been a novelist both burdened and blessed with a highly developed sense of the realities—to say nothing of the madness—of the existing social world. He has also struggled to find in those realities meanings that reach beyond the secular, that will support and validate an essentially metaphysical view of human experience. This suggests that Bellow's imagination is dialectical and is always engaged in a debate between the secular and the transcendental, a debate he can carry on because he is almost alone among contemporary American novelists in having the power to tolerate, without collapsing under the stress of, philosophical ambiguity. And he has, in turn, found this possible because he is a man of great intellectual vitality who has consistently been willing, like Mailer but in marked contrast to Styron, to risk his career by venturing, with each new book, beyond the imaginative territories he has previously explored and consolidated. Where most writers take possession of their subjects, along with the technical means to engage them, fairly early in life and then proceed gradually to exhaust them, Bellow from the beginning has maintained a much more flexible and dynamic relation with the materials of his art, and he has brought to their service an intellectual culture far more extensive than that of his American contemporaries. Ideas for him are not only a primary basis of subject matter, nor are they—as so much of our literature seems to imply—antithetical to the expression of honest feeling and the actualities of "real" life. Rather, they serve to broaden and intensify his perception of those actualities, and they help him to dramatize what he sees as the vital connections, so complexly explored in all his novels, between worldly experience and the abstracting transcendences of history, morality, philosophy, and religion.

Bellow also has the capacity—very nearly as rare among our novelists as the power of abstract thought—to experiment with a variety of novelistic techniques in which to cast his continuously evolving conception of his materials. From time to time and often within the limits of a single book he has made brilliant use of the effects of naturalist realism, the comedy of manners, black humor, the mystery novel, the picaresque, psychological, and philosophical novel, and literary satire (in *Henderson the Rain King*, partly a parody of the mythic narrative of descent into the heart of darkness), and his virtuosity has been reinforced by his very considerable knowledge of American and European literature, philosophy, and psychology. Jung, Wilhelm Reich, Rudolf Steiner, Sartre, Dostoevsky, Dickens, Melville, Whitman, and Mark Twain have all been prominent influences on Bellow, but as is the case with most major novelists, he has not so much imitated as transmuted certain of their features to fit the requirements of his imagination. His indebtednesses, however, are often obvious, and sometimes they are flagrant. For example, his first novel, *Dangling Man*, appears to have been strongly influenced by Sartre's *Nausea,* and the protagonist bears a close resemblance —as, for that matter, do so many characters in post-modern fiction—to Dostoevsky's Underground Man. *The Victim* is also derivative of Dostoevsky, as Bellow himself admitted in an interview he gave in 1964: in terms of sheer plot, it is virtually a retelling of *The Eternal Husband. The Adventures of Augie March,* the third and most ambitious of Bellow's early novels, is a mélange of styles, characters, dramatic episodes, and literary echoes, and as it represents a radical departure from the tight, highly formalized works with which he began his career, so it marks at least a temporary turning away from European in favor of native American influences—Whitman, Twain, Dreiser, and just possibly Melville.

Augie March was and remains Bellow's great transitional work, an expression of manic energy and high comedic talent he had not previously been able to release, a kind of fiction sufficiently open and flexible to allow him for the first time to do absolutely anything he chose, in which he was freed rather than inhibited by the technical requirements of his medium. Ever since, Bellow has been experimenting with new arrangements and combinations of forms and styles, different angles of approach to materials which were all essentially present in *Augie March* but which, in his subsequent novels, needed to be processed according to the dictates of his maturing perceptions of experience. *Henderson the Rain King* is basically a mock-heroic rendering of Augie's quest for self-knowledge. Henderson's flight into Africa, where he becomes a buffoon fertility god among primitive tribes and finally believes or *decides* to believe he has discovered himself, burlesques Augie's flight from the various "reality instructors" who want to educate him in their distorted visions of the world.

With *Herzog,* in the writer of unmailed letters to prominent people, the Underground Man reappears. The sufferer who seeks after goodness and wisdom is once again the farcical martyr persecuted by malevolent would-be teachers, and in the end he breaks out into freedom and peace or—depending on one's interpretation of the closing scenes—he capitulates to his situation and to himself as he is, saying, "I am pretty well satisfied to be, to be just as it is willed, for as long as I may remain in occupancy . . ."—a note of complacent resignation that, as I once wrote, seems falsely imposed and that calls into question the authenticity of the novel's narrative voice.

Finally in *Mr. Sammler's Planet*, the novel just preceding *Humboldt's Gift*, the sufferer, now an old man bewildered and put upon by the anarchy of life in the contemporary city, searches for some understanding of the ultimate purpose of human existence, some knowledge that will enable him to accept the fact of his nephew's and his own imminent death as well as, conceivably, the eventual extinction of human life on earth. In a fashion that becomes increasingly evident in Bellow's later protagonists, Mr. Sammler moves from self-preoccupation and secular intellectuality closer and closer to mysticism, seeking what one critic has called "the Tolstoyan moment," the instant of apocalyptic perception in which the patterns unifying the cosmos and linking man to the cosmos become visible and comprehensible.

However dissimilar they may be in other respects, Bellow's novels all tell essentially the same story. They are all informed by what can only be called a *desperately* affirmative view of human experience and possibility, a view too complicated to be reducible to a philosophical proposition, too dialectical and contradictory to be taken as dogma, creed, or panacea. Its central feature is, in fact, ambiguity, a recognition of elements that may be forever irreconcilable, of questions that must be pondered and explored, but for which answers will probably never be found, at least not by the merely human creatures who seek them. Bellow on several occasions has expressed his strong disagreement with the idea of cultural nihilism and alienation that pervades so much of modern and contemporary literature and that he believes has its source far more *in* literature than in the actual life it purports to reflect. As he said in his Library of Congress address in 1963:

> Writers have inherited a tone of bitterness from the great poems and novels of this century, many of which lament the passing of a more stable and beautiful age demolished by the barbarous intrusion of an industrial and metropolitan society

of masses or proles who will, after many upheavals, be tamed by bureaucracies and oligarchies in brave new worlds, human anthills. . . . There are modern novelists who take all this for granted as fully proven and implicit in the human condition and who complain as steadily as they write, viewing modern life with a bitterness to which they themselves have not established clear title, and it is this unearned bitterness I speak of.

Herzog, in one of his unmailed letters to his friend Shapiro, angrily denounced "the commonplaces of the Wasteland outlook, the cheap mental stimulants of Alienation, the cant and rant of pipsqueaks about inauthenticity and forlornness. I can't accept this foolish dreariness. We are talking about the whole life of mankind. The subject is too great, too deep for such weakness, cowardice—too deep, too great, Shapiro."

Clearly, Bellow wishes to offer in his fiction a view of modern life that will be alternative to "the commonplaces of the Waste-land outlook," for he has said elsewhere that "a man should have at least sufficient power to overcome ignominy and to complete his own life. His suffering, feebleness, servitude then have a meaning," and it is the writer's duty to affirm that meaning, to "reveal the greatness of man." This Bellow has steadily tried to achieve. He has celebrated life with remarkable vigor, and he has created some of the most compassionate portraits of the human condition—even in its thoroughly detestable manifesta-tions—to be found anywhere in contemporary literature. Yet the ultimate revelation of the greatness of man has eluded him, partly because it is much easier artistically to represent evil than to find the terms for the convincing display of virtue, but mostly because Bellow has been thwarted by the very complexity and ambiguity of his view of man.

His problem is that as a writer of great perceptiveness and intellectual honesty he cannot help but be aware and reflect his awareness of all those elements in contemporary life to which the only sane response is despair, which have produced the climate of pessimism and generalized forlornness he finds so oppressive. His moral impulse is to affirm life in some perhaps transcendental way that will be commensurate with his sincere belief in human possibility. But the observable facts of life as it now exists not only afford no proof of that possibility, but seem to work actively to nullify it. Bellow has thus found himself in a position of wishing to believe amid conditions that do not provide adequate objective justifications for belief, and the consequence for his fiction is that it has tended to break apart into two kinds of dramatic statement, which may be developed concurrently, but which cannot be plausibly reconciled. On the one hand, there is material—usually of a speculative, philosophical, or mystical nature—which expresses Bellow's faith that man can attain self-understanding and transformation, that he can overcome the limitations of his individuality, and that he can come into some recognition of his place in the social and cosmic order. On the other hand, there is the far more abundant and vital material which portrays man's cruelty, duplicity, venality, maniacal self-obsessiveness, and hateful determination to exploit others in any way he can in order to prosper in a world where material value is the only value, where success is measured by the standards of the con-game, and where the reigning morality is a cynicism Bellow aptly calls "deceit without guilt."

It may be because Bellow cannot bring into single dramatic focus his optimism about man and his pessimism about the conditions of contemporary life that his characters so often seem schizophrenic and the endings of his novels disappointingly equivocal. His protagonists are men of good will and high hopes who make their way through a hellish wasteland in which they are forced to suffer every imaginable kind of humiliation and injustice. Yet at the end in spite of everything they are still seekers and believers. Martyred and persecuted though they may be, they remain pure and hopeful, still expecting transformation and revelation—perhaps in quiet confidence like Herzog, "well satisfied to be . . . just as it is willed," or like Augie, laughing at nature because "it thinks it can win over us and the power of hope," or like Henderson who, during a stopover in Newfoundland, gets out of the airplane that is bringing him home from Africa and, believing he has at last begun to find his life, runs in ecstasy, an orphaned child in his arms, "over the pure white lining of the gray Arctic silence." These are all endings that represent cessations of narrative action, but not conclusions, pauses in flight, but not the attainment of thematic destination.

In *Humboldt's Gift*, his eighth novel, Bellow had still not found a way of successfully reconciling these contradictory attitudes and the two kinds of material in which they are expressed. But he did manage to cope with them more effectively than he had been able to do in any of his previous novels. The protagonist, Charles Citrine, confirms one's impression that Bellow's views of the nature of human existence are becoming increasingly mystical and may eventually find a formally religious framework. Citrine is a student of Rudolf Steiner's anthroposophy, a doctrine that maintains that, through self-discipline, cognitional experience of the spiritual world can be achieved, and his meditations on such a possibility become a significant yet unobtrusive leitmotif of the novel. But the critical point is that Bellow treats them throughout as meditations only. They are not required to bear a major thematic weight as are the speculative materials in the earlier novels. Therefore, Bellow's inability to reconcile them with his secular materials does not become problematical, since Citrine merely retreats from time to time into his meditations and at best only holds out hope that they may eventually lead him to a perception of spiritual truth.

This is to say that for the first time in this novel Bellow has been able to objectify his own wishful optimism and to accept it for just that, wishful, declining now to try to give it more crucial thematic importance than it can justifiably be given. Citrine emerges as, in other respects, a typical Bellow protagonist, but one who has a mystical turn of mind. He may be another seeker after cosmic understanding but that role is deemphasized because he is first and foremost a suffering victim whose journey through the purgatory of humiliation and betrayal is easily separable from his spiritual pilgrimage. He is therefore placed, with a minimum of distracting metaphysical encumbrances, at the center of the kind of action Bellow has always been able to dramatize with the greatest effectiveness, the action of relentlessly secular existence, and that is surely an important reason why Citrine comes to seem the most convincingly drawn of Bellow's major characters.

As the author of several works of popular biography and a successful Broadway play, Citrine is prosperous and well known, but has reached an impasse in his life and career. His work has gone stale. He has been through a divorce and is being hounded by his ex-wife who, he is convinced, is determined to ruin him financially. He has lawyers who seem to be trying to assist her in this effort in every way they can, and a few friends who may or may not be any more trustworthy. His beautiful mistress is pressuring him to marry her, but since she seriously doubts that he is a man of responsibility, she takes the precaution of sleeping from time to time with a wealthy undertaker.

Because of these and other problems Citrine has withdrawn more and more into himself, spending days at a time alone in his apartment meditating on such matters as the fate of the soul after death and the possibilities of reincarnation. He is also obsessed with the memory of the dead poet Von Humboldt Fleischer, the closest friend and literary mentor of his youth, a creative force of immense size, but a talent destroyed by neglect, eccentricity, paranoia, and alcohol. Fleischer has died alone in poverty and obscurity, and Citrine ponders his life trying to understand its significance, wishing he had been a better friend to Fleischer, regretting that he cannot carry on his work or in some way redeem his reputation.

Then all sorts of dreadful things begin to happen to Citrine and, in the fashion of contemporary black literature of the absurd, they simply happen at the behest of whatever agencies of capricious fatality govern the universe. One of Citrine's friends, troubled by his isolated existence, insists that he take part in a poker game where he will have a chance to meet people who belong to the real world. During the game Citrine drinks too much, babbles about his personal problems, fails to notice that he is being cheated by some of the players, and writes a check to cover his losses. When the next day he stops payment on the check, he is threatened by a small-time Mafia figure named Cantabile, who takes his revenge by arranging to have Citrine's $18,000 Mercedes 280-SL clubbed to ruin in the street. Cantabile then forces Citrine to make an apology before witnesses for defaulting on the debt, and when Citrine offers him cash, he humiliates Citrine further by again forcing him to accompany him, this time to the top story of a skyscraper under construction. There, on a swaying catwalk high above the city, Cantabile takes the fifty-dollar bills Citrine has given him, folds them into paper airplanes, and sails them off into the wind.

These persecutions, as it turns out, are merely initiatory. A short time later a district judge decides that Citrine must pay his ex-wife an amount of money that will virtually wipe him out and then orders him to post a bond of $200,000. Nevertheless, Citrine goes off on a long-planned trip to Europe where he expects to be joined by his mistress. But while waiting for her in Madrid, he learns that she has gone to Italy and married the undertaker—the betrayal having evidently been carefully plotted from the moment it became apparent that Citrine was no longer a good financial prospect. Left alone in Madrid, he resumes his meditations on the occult and experiments with trying to communicate with the spirits of the dead, in particular with Fleischer. The experiments fail, but in a remarkable way. Fleischer finally does communicate with Citrine and passes on to him his gift or legacy. The proceeds from it will not make Citrine rich, but they will help him begin life again, and he supposes it will be a radically different kind of life, a cessation of struggle, extravagance, self-loathing, and boredom, an attempt to "listen in secret to the sound of the truth that God puts into us."

Described in this way the action in its details may seem trivial or merely ludicrous. It is surely not redeemed by the metaphysical dimension nor is the ending altogether satisfactory. But the power of the novel derives in the Jamesean sense from the quality and intensity of the felt life contained within it, the brilliant evocation of the social world, and the incredible sensitivity of its characterizations. It is here rather than in his philosophical assertions that Bellow expresses most forcefully his belief in life and the greatness of man. If he has so far failed to achieve a synthesis of his metaphysical and his secular materials, the failure may, after all, be fortunate. For we expect a novelist to be a chronicler, not a visionary, an observer and analyst, not a seer. In searching for and never quite achieving an understanding of the secret cohering principle of human existence, Bellow has given us a portrait of existence that may contain as much understanding as we can tolerate.

These four writers—Lurie, Baldwin, Mailer, and Bellow—have each tried to engage with some honesty and realism the materials to be found in contemporary American society. And each has experienced frustration or the need to make some creative adjustment or compromise in the face of the recalcitrance of those materials. The problem for Lurie is her inadequate comprehension of the ambiguities underlying the current academic scene as well as the changes in manners and morals that have rendered that scene very nearly impenetrable to the novelist whose imagination cannot break free of the cliché formulations of the past. Baldwin's curse is the sentimentality of his vision of the black experience. Mailer, through the discovery of materials congenial to his talents in the political and social crises of the sixties, also discovered his style and his individual voice and a way of using himself as a chief character in the scenes of his reportage. Bellow may not yet have achieved a reconciliation of his transcendental and his secular interests. But all these writers have chosen to make the effort to confront and cope imaginatively with the prevailing social realities or unrealities—Bellow and Mailer most successfully—rather than resort to the creation of metaphors or parables intended to represent the human predicament in our time but also representing the retreat of realism in the face of that predicament.

CHAPTER VIII

The Novel as Narcissus

As for art, it not only fails to create the illusion of reality but suffers from the same crisis of self-consciousness that afflicts the man in the street. Novelists and playwrights call attention to the artificiality of their own creations and discourage the reader from identifying with the characters. By means of irony and eclecticism, the writer withdraws from his subject but at the same time becomes so conscious of these distancing techniques that he finds it more and more difficult to write about anything except the difficulty of writing.

—Christopher Lasch

One of the most prominent manifestations of this retreat is the development over the last twenty years of the kind of fiction Robert Scholes has called "fabulation," a term he used to describe —in some cases with only approximate precision—the work of novelists who are committed to anti-realism and who are trying to create—insofar as it is ever possible—an almost wholly self-contained fiction. This is a fiction which derives its meaning and justification only slightly from its mimetic or impressionistic relation to a known actuality and almost entirely from its parodical treatment of past literary conventions, the thematic correspondences established among its internal parts, its use of violent and at times fantastic or inexplicable occurrences, the ironic and grotesque quality of its language and imagery, and the arbitrary and often interchangeable identities of its characters, who often appear to have been modeled on one-dimensional comic-strip figures or the heroes and villains of boys' adventure stories. These features all suggest that fiction of this kind may be considered fabulation not in the sense that it states an explicit moral or follows the pattern of allegory, but rather in the sense that it attempts to create an impression or hallucination of the fabulous nature of contemporary reality and, by implication, of the current blurring of distinction between reality and fiction.

That, at any rate, may be one explanation for the fact that this is above all a fiction supremely conscious of itself in the process of coming into being and heavily weighted by evidence of the author's struggle to separate what is true from what is illusory or delusional in his solipsistic field of vision. As such, it undoubtedly represents an inevitable extension into literature of that preoccupation with self that is the chief feature of contemporary life as well as a symptom of just how difficult it is to cope with and comprehend contemporary life. The self becomes the one reality that may be more or less dependably known, and for the writers of fabulative fiction it seems to be the one reality from which they cannot escape. In the somewhat hortatory manner of some of their predecessors in the eighteenth century, they will periodically intrude themselves upon their narratives to inform the reader that he is reading a fiction and that the author is having a hard time writing it. At one such moment in *The Exagggerations of Peter Prince*, Steve Katz admonishes himself as author, saying, "Enough! Katz, you're making this all up," and later he complains that "writing this book is like trying to hug a plastic cleaning sack . . . stuffed with Jello." Then there is the novel—Richard Brautigan's *A Confederate General from Big Sur* is a well-known example—to which the author offers several alternative endings and invites the reader to choose the one best suited to his taste. Or, as happens in John Barth's *Giles Goat-Boy* and Gilbert Sorrentino's *Mulligan Stew*, the author may open his narrative with elaborate mock-historical prefaces containing ostensibly genuine publishers' letters giving their reasons for declining to publish the novel that follows, or there may be prefatory assertions that the person whose name appears on the title page did not in fact write the novel but that, in the case of *Giles Goat-Boy*, it was composed by a man named Stoker Giles or Giles Stoker, or it may even have been written by a computer.

Carried to its ultimate extreme, this belief in the interchangeability of reality and fiction can lead to an arrogant disrespect for the integrity of both. The author becomes contemptuous of the fact that he is making up characters and situations that are not, after all, "real" and finds a perverse pleasure in manipulating them at whim or destroying them whenever they cease to hold his interest—as if taking revenge on his medium for being no longer bound by the conventions of realism and so permitting him to take whatever liberties he chooses.

Sorrentino, one of Barth's more obvious imitators, is an excellent example of this tendency. In *Mulligan Stew* his protagonist, Antony Lamont, is a novelist engaged in writing a novel that is of course *Mulligan Stew*. *His* two main characters are not only writing novels of their own as well as journals and letters, but *know* that they are characters in Lamont's novel and from time to time discuss the meaning of the situations in which he has placed them. They also converse with other people who are in fact professional characters in novels written by other novelists, and they both carry on a love affair with Daisy Buchanan, wife of wealthy sportsman Tom Buchanan—two superstar characters of the modern novelistic canon. What little action there is in the novel is carried forward through the relationship with Daisy, but is constantly interrupted so that Sorrentino-Lamont can insert long Joycean inventories of the contents of bookcases, pornographic masques and parodies reminiscent of the Circe episode in *Ulysses*, and senseless catechistic interrogations in the manner of the Ithaca episode in *Ulysses*—all of which appear to be intended to dramatize the pointlessness of what is going on, the completely arbitrary nature of the fiction-making process when one has no faith in the possibility of achieving any meaning whatsoever.

These various intrusions, conceits, and prevarications are all seemingly meant to suggest that indeed there no longer exists a dependable way of separating fact from fiction or the genuine author from the pseudo-author, that a great deal of contemporary fact is so outlandish and absurd that it appears to be, and might as well be, fictitious, that all fictions are simply versions of what is undoubtedly an unknowable truth, that, therefore, one version may be considered as valid as any other, and that finally the only thing we can be reasonably certain is real is the author contriving his particular and highly provisional version out of the depths of his own endlessly equivocating self.

John Barth, the most prominent and gifted of the writers of fabulation, became obsessed early in his career—as did Pynchon—by an idea about the nature of the cosmos: namely, that no idea about it can be securely held since everything is relative and there are no absolute truths or fixed realities. Each person has only his version or versions of the truth; hence, each can, if he is so inclined, live his life by improvising and playing a seemingly limitless series of roles that may be external public expressions of the various versions of the truth he perceives as he makes his adjustments to new experience.

Barth's first two novels were relatively realistic dramatic explorations of this idea. *The Floating Opera* has to do with Todd Andrews's decision to commit suicide, but then how he changes his mind when he perceives that while there is no rational reason to live, there is also no rational reason to die. It is significant for what it suggests about Barth's quite mechanistic view of human motivation that Andrews presents the evolution of his decision and his change of mind in the form of a series of dialectical propositions:

I. Nothing has intrinsic value.
II. The reasons for which people attribute value to things are always ultimately irrational.
III. There is, therefore, no ultimate "reason" for valuing anything.
IV. Living is action. There's no final reason for action.
V. There's no final reason for living (or for suicide).

These insights are apparently all that Andrews has been able to derive from the experience of his life by which he can justify its continuance or its termination. But then Andrews has lived a life unstructured and unenriched by any imperative except a free-floating compulsion to rationalize. He is almost entirely immune to emotional stimuli and to the perhaps irrational, but nonetheless vitalizing human relationships that make existence tolerable for most people. The single compelling need of his life, he insists, is to understand why his father committed suicide. But the only means he has of trying to penetrate this mystery is to put down on paper everything he knows about his father and to infer from the accumulation of data what his father's motives may have been. Of course he fails in the endeavor because all his efforts to fabricate systems and patterns of action turn out to be only possible versions of the truth, and since he himself is so isolated from life, these versions serve only to propel him further away from life and to seal the vacuum of solipsism in which he spends his days—literally in the hotel room where for many years he has lived alone with his infinitely ramifying and self-sabotaging mind.

Barth's second novel, *End of the Road*, explores the human consequences of this philosophical dilemma, just what happens when a person who is victimized by it as Andrews is becomes involved in the lives of other people. Jacob Horner, the protagonist, suffers from periods of catatonic paralysis or what he calls "weatherlessness," in which he is unable to take any action because his psyche is balked by the massive plentitude of possibilities for action. While trying to recover from one of these periods, Horner drifts into a friendship with Joe and Rennie Morgan, a young couple who believe they can live their lives by rules based upon reason and practical sanity. With very little passionate volition on the part of either, Horner and Rennie have an affair which leads not only to the destruction of the Morgans' marriage, but to a particularly gruesome death for Rennie while she is undergoing an abortion. Joe is left in a condition of complete metaphysical breakdown because he is unable to arrive at a rational way of understanding the situation. "According to my version of Rennie, what happened couldn't have happened. According to her version of herself, it couldn't have happened. And yet it happened." Horner at the end still cannot believe in any version of reality and appears to be entering yet another period of paralysis that may well be, as the last word of the novel suggests, "terminal."

Both these novels are, as I have said, quite realistic examinations of the dilemma created by the failure of logical systems to provide a tenable basis for existence and of the resulting entrapment of the will in a bottomless quagmire of relativism. One derives the strong impression that in writing them Barth had himself arrived at a point of imaginative development or depletion at which, like his protagonists, he could no longer find real or meaningful any of the conventional methods of cohering experience that are so essential not only to the rational maintenance of life, but also to the production of realistic fiction. In fact, both books are finally *about* the impossibility of arriving at any secure perspective from which to judge human affairs; their realism is always on the verge of being nullified by their epistemological resistance to the premises of realism. Obviously, this is a clear declaration of impasse for the novelist unless he is able to discover some means of converting the very elements of the impasse *into* his subject matter, while at the same time turning away as completely as possible from materials drawn from the contemporary social scene that require specific realistic treatment.

It was perhaps logical, therefore, that Barth in his well-known essay, "The Literature of Exhaustion," should announce the obsolescence of all the conventions of the realistic novel—"cause and effect, linear anecdote, characterization, authorial selection, arrangement, and interpretation" (conventions that have formed the basis of our conception of the novel from the beginnings of its history) and insist that the only worthwhile function for the novelist at the present time is to parody those conventions, to produce "imitations-of-novels, which attempt to represent not life directly but a representation of life" or, ultimately, "something like *The Sotweed Factor* or *Giles Goat-Boy*: novels which imitate the form of the Novel, by an author who imitates the role of Author."

Barth's implication here is that whether through the exhaustion of the realistic genre, his own imaginative exhaustion and boredom with the overly familiar effects of a worked-out tradition, or the impossibility of giving adequate expression to current social actualities within the formalized modes of that tradition, the novelist today has no choice but to focus his attention on the fiction-making process itself. He must create complication and mystery not through the exploration of human character, but rather through an ironic or parodic manipulation of his fictive resources within the closed precincts of any given novel— the relation between his imagined reality and public social reality being no longer imitative but at most metaphorical or surrealistic or even finally altogether indefinable and, for that matter, altogether irrelevant.

What Barth in fact does in both *The Sotweed Factor* and *Giles Goat-Boy* is transfer his paralyzing idea of "versions" from the situation of characters like Andrews and Horner to the interior of his fiction, where "versions" become not the differing and conflicting perspectives the characters bring to the depicted actions, but rather the conflicting ways in which Barth the novelist *does* the depicting. Where for Andrews and Horner "versions" were a prime cause of psychological impasse, they now become dramatic expressions of the author's imaginative impasse. After Barth has put before us a bewildering variety of possible approaches to, and interpretations of, the many events of his narrative and then requires them to undercut and neutralize one another, nothing solid is finally left. All the "versions" have been rendered suspect, leaving the reader to conclude that there is no way at all that reality can be engaged, that, in fact, there is no reality other than the self-canceling efforts of the author to discover that there is none. In this sense *The Sotweed Factor* and *Giles Goat-Boy*, ingenious though they may be in conception, are novels made to self-destruct—the one being an imitation and parody of an eighteenth-century picaresque novel in which Barth endlessly invokes the authority of history only to nullify that authority by exposing it as merely another version of an unfathomable truth, the other being a mock-epic and comic burlesque of the stereotypical heroic quest in which such figures as Jesus Christ, Oedipus, and John F. Kennedy are deflated and trivialized into farce by a vigorously enforced reductive angle of vision that allows no character or occurrence within the novel to possess more than a momentary and provisional validity.

In *Lost in the Funhouse*, his collection of more or less thematically related short stories, Barth emerges as the author so obsessively conscious of the possible ways of presenting his narrative that finally all possibilities are sabotaged and the very idea of narrative becomes unthinkable. In the title story, which is preceded by a few quite excellent stories done, surprisingly enough, in a fairly conventional realistic manner, a family spends the Fourth of July at an amusement park, and a thirteen-year-old boy either does or does not get lost in the funhouse, while Barth interrupts the action regularly to discuss alternative ways of carrying it forward. The funhouse is of course an objectification of his vision of life in its baffling relation to the artist, but the bafflement is in fact the story. The protagonist is not the boy, but rather John Barth demonstrating why the boy can never enter the funhouse or find his way out of it, become either lost or found, be brought to life as a character or made to enter life as a human being. The funhouse with its infinitely magnifying hall of mirrors and labyrinthine passageways leading to illusory dead ends is the culminating image of Barth's own imaginative dead end, the exhaustion of his sense of creative possibility, his ultimate capitulation before the challenge of utterance, and in the story called "Anonymiad" he confesses his defeat: "I yearned to be relieved of myself. . . . I'd relapse into numbness, as if, having abandoned song for speech, I meant now to give up language altogether and float voiceless in the wash of time like an amphora in the sea, my vision bottled."

The only alternative for the writer who has thought himself beyond the limits of narrative possibility is silence, and an insistent yearning to become silent, in effect to kill himself off as an articulating artist, can be felt throughout Barth's more recent work. But in the epistolary novel called *Letters*, he seems to have tried for a brief postponement of suicide by retreating completely into the bottled vision of his previous novels and carrying on an imaginary correspondence with the many characters he created in those novels—or he will have them correspond with one another. Jacob Horner is brought forward to tell—in a letter addressed fittingly to himself in his earlier incarnation in *End of the Road*—what happened to him after the conclusion of that novel. Barth as the author of *Letters* writes to Tod Andrews to ask him if he would be willing to appear as a character in a new work of fiction that will become *Letters*, and even to serve as Barth's attorney in the event that any libel suits should result from the novel's publication. Tod Andrews writes an annual death-day letter to his deceased father, telling him of the resumption of his affair with Jane Mack—that relationship having been terminated by Jane at the end of *The Floating Opera*.

By establishing in this way a series of incestuous relationships with his own fictional progeny, Barth relieves himself of having to create new characters. He is not required to invent alternative ways of presenting his narrative because "reality" has already been established as fixed by the manner in which it was presented in the earlier novels. And that fictional reality has become a substitute for the world of extra-fictional reality, which now need not be consulted at all, since the fiction is all there is. All that is important has occurred in the novels and not in life, while life has been totally fictionalized by the novels. Barth, in his turn, has disappeared as author into his creation and become, like his characters, a fictional version of a hypothetical human being. His vision has indeed become bottled and he voiceless in the wash of his previous vision, an amphora whose only function is to be a surviving artifact of a function he himself has rendered obsolete.

Barth once remarked that "reality is a nice place to visit but you wouldn't want to live there. . . . Reality is a drag." The fictional method which he has been steadily elaborating ever since he published *End of the Road* has enabled him not only to avoid living in reality, but also to escape having even to pay it a visit. The extreme internalization of all those technical effects, which in the work of a realistic novelist would serve as mimetic or at most metaphorical points of exit to the external world, has resulted in a fiction that sustains itself almost entirely through the consumption of its own entrails. The complex, cross-indexed system of allusions to events and characters that exist solely within the novel that is in process of being written or the novels that have previously been written, the introduction of mythical figures as well as actual historical personages into a context in which they are taken apart and reassembled so as to serve the purposes of a Barthian anti-myth—all make it possible for Barth to avoid the immensely difficult problem of having to confront the complexities of the external world. One can remain lost in the funhouse forever and endlessly contemplate the myriad distortions of one's reflection in the hall of mirrors and endlessly speculate on the meaning of those distortions—or on whether they have meaning. And all the while one can be safe from the intrusion of any reality that is not itself one of the distortions, a product of the mirrored scene.

Yet for better or worse, the world outside the funhouse is where the novelist must begin, even if he ends in a world that represents only a fictive version of the outside world. But when the connection between the world and its version is broken or was never made in the first place, then the version is no longer a version but has become its own subject, while the author has appointed himself the observer of the process by which the subject has become the subject and he the observer of the process. The ultimate result, as Barth's recent work makes clear, is that the author becomes trapped in the act of creation with a steadily diminishing awareness of just what the materials are that the act was meant to create. Clearly, they should be something more than the materials of creation themselves. The pot of paint and the canvas are not, after all, the painting. But then if Barth believes that the reality that might be painted is a bore, he has no choice other than to make what he can of the emptiness of his canvas.

CHAPTER IX

Living and Partly Living

The development—if that it can be called—from self-preoccupation as a pervasive psychic condition of our society to novels that are specifically *about* self-preoccupation reaches its logical culmination in novels that are themselves self-preoccupied—it being apparently the case that the overriding concerns of a culture at any particular time in history will find their reflection, however obliquely, in the kinds of fiction the culture produces. If, furthermore, we have, at one extreme, novels whose subject is self-preoccupation and, at the other extreme, novels whose subject is preoccupation with themselves, then it may well be that we are discovering only that the coin of narcissism has, in fact, two sides. Novels of the first sort seem to be saying that nothing is real or important except the self and the processes by which it has become obsessively aware of this fact. Novels of the second sort seem to be saying—even belligerently proclaiming—that nothing is real or important except *them*selves and the processes by which, as artistic constructs, they were created—including of course the authors' lamentations over the bewildering variety of alternative ways in which they *might* have been created. John Barth's assertion that reality is a bore and, therefore, does not deserve to be treated in fiction—since only the techniques of fiction perceived *in vacuo* merit that honor—is merely a restatement in other terms of the widespread belief that experience outside the familiar and beloved precincts of the self—whether as person or as novel—is irrelevant, trivial, too incoherent and grotesque to be understandable, and indeed very probably a bore as well.

Such a belief, in whatever terms it is phrased, would seem to prophesy, even herald, the imminent extinction of the novel as a medium for making a realistic statement about the nature of our collective social experience, just as the arbitrary and often quite cynical use of the "versions" approach to experience would seem to express a fatal loss of respect for the integrity of both experience and the novel form. Yet it might be argued that much that passes for reality in the contemporary world *is* in fact a bore—as is, inevitably, so much of the fiction that reflects its boringness or turns away from reflecting it because of boredom. The self as a person or as a novel contemplating his, her, or its own intimate processes is deemed by the writers of such fiction to be all that remains worthy of their regard, even as we recognize that there are others like Bellow and Mailer whose work stands in strong rebuttal to this assumption.

The question of just how the assumption has achieved the considerable authority it now enjoys has been a recurring, at times subliminal preoccupation of this book. If the personal self is now widely perceived to be the sole remaining bastion of reality, if the novel is now widely perceived to be the maker of the only reality that counts—that is, itself—then clearly there are conditions in our society that have forced the personal self and the novel into a most radical state of beleaguerment.

Among them we must first count the obvious: the enormous power of the mass communications media to shape our vision— indeed, to *become* our vision—of the nature and meaning of experience. We have constantly available to us the most extensive information about the great macrocosmic issues of our time— worldwide terrorism, the proliferation of nuclear arms, ravagement of the environment by radioactive waste, the blackmail of governments by the Middle Eastern oil-producing countries. Most of us are undoubtedly much better informed about events occurring in Iran, however mystifying they may be, than we are about what goes on in the households of our most intimate friends. Thus, events in the macrocosm of world affairs have been given an importance, arising out of the sheer volume of information we possess about them, that is not conferred upon the microcosmic world of family, friends, and community. Yet because what we have is *information* rather than direct personal experience of these events, because they are not, as a rule, happening to us or to anyone we know, but come to us only through the media that convey the news that they are happening elsewhere, our response to them is equivocal. On the one hand, they seem vastly important because we know so much about them. On the other, they seem abstract and impersonal because they do not belong, and cannot be made to belong, to our immediate experience. In addition, many of the events and problems that threaten the world have such horrendous implications that they become unimaginable and cause us to retreat into a self-protective lethargy in order to avoid confronting their reality.

Another factor leading to a further diminishment of our perception of experience is that the life we lead in relation to others, the life that was once a primary source of both stability and dramatic conflict, has itself come to seem remote and oddly unreal, as if it were no longer quite in our possession or under our control. This has occurred not only because our relations with others as well as with ourselves may justifiably seem trivial when compared with the magnitude of world events, but because these relations have been quite literally depersonalized through the operations of social and psychiatric technology, the processes by which all human concerns, whether they involve satisfactory sexual performance, making optimum use of one's talents, or getting along harmoniously with others, are removed from the unsafe keeping of the individuals struggling to cope with them and placed in the custody of the various human-engineering agencies for the proper therapy and consultation, for treatment as "cases" that are common to many and, therefore, that need not be dealt with by the isolated suffering self. Through a slight variation of the same process, whole masses of people who may once have endured miserable persecuted or impoverished lives are now organized into social collectives and vigorously lobby for their rights, appealing to the higher courts of legislative manipulation for redress of collective injustices that formerly had to be engaged personally. However beneficial this may be to the health of society, its effect has been to disinfect human existence of much of its dramatic and tragic potential and to trivialize, if not altogether tranquilize, conflicts that not so very long ago provided our novelists with some of their most vital materials. In fact, the classic story told again and again by such modern writers of social realism as Dreiser, Dos Passos, Steinbeck, and Farrell was essentially the story of sensitive and often gifted people struggling for survival and fulfillment against the pressures of a provincially oppressive or underprivileged society and, as a rule, living to discover that the struggle has forced them to compromise or corrupt the innocent idealism with which they began. If a social-services agency or an equal-rights lobby had been available to Jennie Gerhardt, Carrie Meeber, Clyde Griffiths, or Studs Lonigan, they might have arrived at a different and better end. But the victory would have belonged to sociology and politics and not to literature.

In television and the many films manufactured for the popular audience one encounters a puerile fantasy version of the prevailing view of life as an experience that can be cured by the application of the proper manipulative techniques. The problems addressed by these media are usually classifiable under the headings of romantic or sexual discord arising between lovers and spouses, the anxieties produced by crippling and often eventually fatal physical disorders (cancer, muscular dystrophy, brain tumor, and the multiple loss of limbs being among the most common), the terrors produced as a result of the invasion of ordinary, decent lives by diabolical supernatural beings, or the invasion of ordinary, decent lives by diabolical secular beings bent upon rape, pillage, and torture. What is of interest is that the melodrama in such cases rarely focuses on the quality of suffering engendered by a particular disaster or on the role played by the disaster in illuminating the character of the sufferer. It also exists without relation to such basic human issues as conflict of moral principle and ideology, conscience at odds with expediency, the complex nature of the motivation that may determine conduct, the even more complex nature of personal relationships that are necessarily affected in a fundamental way by the social and historical milieu in which they are carried on. These essential elements of real-life existence have no meaning in the media world, and cannot have, because the interest lies not in reality, but in problems that have been concocted for the sole purpose of being solved—the solution engineered, as a rule, through referral of the problems to some neutralizing external authority. The romantic and sexual difficulties are disinfected of drama as well as meaning for the people involved by the resolution that is arranged for them in guidance-counseling and psychoanalysis. The medical difficulties are of course not seen in relation to the suffering endured by the patient, but rather in terms of their cure after a long course of treatment, during which it is the attending physicians who become heroic rather than the patient. The terrors produced by criminal invasion are purged by the timely intervention of the police, whereas those produced by supernatural invasion in themselves represent the displacement of the drama to a transcendental sphere of being that is exempt from all laws of earthly logic.

But the quality of life created as well as reflected by this infantile view of existence is perhaps more accurately characterized by the television commercial than by the programming it interrupts. There all problems are solved by spontaneous consumption—whether of food, beer, cars, or detergents—in an interminable bacchanal of pop-eyed orality. Where the notion of "hand-to-mouth" was once associated with the deprivations of poverty, it now describes the principal activity of poor and affluent alike, and television offers palliative variations on it that entertain the viewer while he is consuming. In soap-opera romance there is the mouth-to-mouth activity of lovers whose kissing has in recent years taken on the appearance of biting and chewing up each other's lips, teeth, and mouth in small wet nibbles of mastication—and there is the hand-to-hand violence of criminals and police officers trying to kill one another: the Dionysiac consumerism of Eros and Thanatos. The blue-collar worker, home from another dead day at the plant, finds momentary relief from his feelings of non-feeling in the joyous abandon of macho destructiveness—the total demolition of cars in freeway collisions or high-speed plunges over the edge of precipices—in which he becomes a fantasy master rather than a real-life minion. The middle-class technocrat finds similar relief in his liberal-sentimental fantasy that the proletariat are able to express emotions of rage or lust that are forbidden to his tidily programmed psyche. For so many of his kind, existence is solely professional life, the obsessive consumption of work being the prime narcosis for their sense that there is really nothing else in this culture worth doing.

One might, in fact, infer from the current dramatic offerings on television—particularly the nighttime serial programs—that the only sources of vital conflict, physical risk, and moral challenge still alive in our society are to be found among the proletariat. The typical daytime soap opera carries forward, at imperceptible pace, a fantasy narrative of largely middle-class intrigues and dismays that possess just enough socially disruptive potential to titillate, but never to threaten an audience to whom no crisis or tragedy in life is conceivable because no problem is conceivable that cannot finally be corrected through arbitration, consultation, or medication. The degree of psychological control required for the maintenance of American middle-class life is such, and the refusal of self-scrutiny is so preposterously great, that only highly censored versions of reality can safely be assimilated by the soap opera audience, only those, in fact, which can be seen to be solvable in ways that will distance them from the unhappy personal situation of any viewer and defuse them of human feeling.

Thus, there is a kind of prim mortician's gloom about the proceedings on soap opera, as if all those small neat adulteries, abortions, miscarriages, cancers, suicides, and murders were not living facts, but rather specimens that had been drained of their vital juices, pickled in formaldehyde, and laid out for the autopsical knife—awaiting the expert opinion as to the causes of, and possible future remedies for these vexing disorders in the otherwise perfectly healthy social corpus. These disorders exist of course in the same metaphysical milieu as the commercials for deodorants and mouth-washes and femine hygiene equipment— sex, sin, and fatal disease all nicely disinfected of rut, sweat, germy wickedness, and death and abstracted into clinical conditions that must be dispassionately analyzed and brought under treatment by the terribly decent people to whom they unaccountably happened.

But come the dark of night and, as if in revenge for this carefully programmed banality, all hell breaks loose. The id blows off the faint authority of the blue-collar superego, the T-shirted furies come ravaging forth, and the orgy of blood begins. There is only one drama in the world of nighttime prole television, and that is the melodrama of physical violence, the chief feature of which is that it is a ritual substitute for the creation of character. In fact, there are no characters as such in prole television, only instantly provoked acts of aggression or retaliation committed by two-legged bunches of ganglia. For, clearly, what the audience demands is not insight but a show of force and the quick *frisson* of omnipotence that comes with hurting and destruction or macho defiance of the police, the kill-joy symbols of the technocratic elite, the anal-retentiveness of property ownership and decorous behavior, the restraint of the impulse to mayhem and murder, the castrated psyche of corporate management. But the brawling truck drivers and construction hard-hats, the drag-racers, and the homocidal drifters self-created out of the ancient Hollywood mythology of the lone-gun outlaw—these are the sainted and hale of groin, the contemporary counterparts of those peasants out of O'Casey and Faulkner who are perfectly at home with their hostilities, rich with the savage wisdom of the flesh, and so are able to respond to what is really real—unlike the middle-class social engineers with their high brows and no loins.

Yet it is of interest that as expressions of manic or psychotic behavior increase in television and film, they seem to decline in the private and public lives of most of us. People in commercials overemote about everything, presumably to compensate for the fact that they have nothing to emote about. The discovery that decaffinated coffee is *real* coffee triggers a reaction of ecstatic wonderment. Grown men and women go gooney over a clean shirt collar—the emotion displayed varying inversely with the emotion aroused by the experience of humdrum daily life.

Similarly, the eroticism in the increasing number of films devoted to the ritualized humiliation and torment of women stands in inverse relation to the actual eroticism—sadistic or otherwise—that appears to be alive in the culture. What one, in fact, notices is a sharp decline of erotic interest between the sexes, at the same time that the media continue to escalate that interest in their fantasy productions. Whether because the shrinkage of the economy has led us unconsciously to avoid the risks of sexual adventure because it is seen as a dangerous incursion on our strained emotional budget or whether because sex has become so technologized an activity that it is no longer a pleasure, but a disagreeable challenge to our powers of gymnastic performance, the truth seems to be that voyeuristic sex has rapidly replaced participatory sex, with the result that a novelist seeking the actual in contemporary experience might well conclude that boredom and indifference are the most common conditions of the public sexual morale, while a fevered vicarious interest that finds little or no expression except in fantasy via masturbation is the pervasive psychological condition.

It is, therefore, not surprising that the individual self—most often the author's very own—should be an obsessive subject of so many of our novels or that there should be so many others that have almost nothing to do with the public social world and, insofar as they are about anything at all, are preoccupied with all the thinkable ways of ringing changes on their own thematic and technical effects. The poverty or vapidity of materials in the public world would appear to make it necessary for the novel, like the mass of the population as a whole, to seek its nourishment in narcissism. It would indeed appear that the mass media are doing our essential living as well as imagining for us. But since the vision of life they present is mostly banal, the emotion counterfeit, and our responses to it vicarious, it is extremely difficult to determine what experience, if any, they finally do reflect. Is it entirely a fiction of their own cynical manufacture, or is it an existing actuality which their fiction faithfully and remorselessly records?

CHAPTER X

Commonplaces of the Wasteland

Yet after making due allowance for these perplexities one recognizes that perhaps the factor most seriously inhibiting our novelists' perceptions of the public world is the institutionalization over the last fifty years of what Saul Bellow has called "the commonplaces of the Wasteland outlook, the cheap mental stimulants of Alienation," the tendency Lionel Trilling once described, far less pejoratively, as the prevailing "anti-cultural bias" of modernist literature. For as long as that literature has existed, its characterizing feature has indeed been a profoundly skeptical, even morosely negative view of established culture and the moral and emotional assumptions on which it is based. Throughout the years of their most vigorous creative activity, nearly all the classic modern novelists, as well as a good many of the poets, saw it as their first responsibility to expose the hypocrisies behind those assumptions, and to crusade for the higher sanctity of spirit that could be achieved only through facing the usually unpleasant truth of the way things actually were. From Flaubert, Joyce, Eliot, Kafka, Lawrence, Céline, Sartre, and Huxley in Europe through Dreiser, Dos Passos, Steinbeck, Farrell, and others in this country, that was the defiant pioneering mission of modernism—to reinvigorate the integrity of the adversary position and, in so doing, to lay down new premises of honesty that would liberate writers from the protective clichés and evasions of the past and enable them to engage the changed realities of the modern age. Inevitably, this honesty was most often expressed in militantly negative terms because it had been achieved against the resistance of a great weight of bourgeois orthodoxy, in opposition to which the modernist reaction could be energized and the degree of its heresy measured.

It is obvious that the negativist view survives today in the many novels that depict contemporary life with the most violent disgust accompanied by the bleakest prognostications of entropy and apocalypse. In fact, the majority of the novelists now considered artistically the most serious appear to take it for granted that adherence to the "Wasteland outlook" is prime evidence of their imaginative integrity, the badge of their membership in the elite corps of revolutionary modernism.

Yet it is also obvious that that outlook has now hardened into a fashionable and highly orthodox mode of vision, that there no longer exists a body of official dogma in opposition to which it might continue to function as a liberating heresy (if only because it is itself the expression of official dogma), and that, therefore, it no longer represents an enlargement of creative perception, but rather a drastic shrinkage.

All this is to say that where the negativist view of classic modernism was an *achieved* view in the sense that it was based on a clear understanding of the suppressed or concealed truths that needed to be exposed and the unjust conditions that required reform, it exists today mainly as a complex of inherited styles and metaphysical assumptions that have largely ceased to have a clear or felt relation to specific experience, but continue to be superimposed on experience in a sort of party-line conformity to an outmoded etiquette of despair, self-hatred, and misanthropy. Indeed, there is much evidence in current fiction to indicate that a writer's need to conform to this etiquette may well determine, even indicate, both his choice of materials and his way of presenting them. Thus, because the negativist view imposes the obligation to be negative, a writer adhering to it will be required to select only those kinds of materials that deserve to be treated negatively, and he will be inclined, perhaps unconsciously, to censor out of his field of vision all those other kinds that require a more sanguine approach. If certain assumptions about the nature of reality become programmatic or totemic, then reality will be forced into conformity with those assumptions.

In the case of the "Wasteland outlook," the image of the modern world as a place of desolation has taken on such authority that it must be maintained however much of a cliché or distortion of the truth it may have become. Hence, it is not surprising that so many of our writers continue to be hypnotized by that image to the point where they have become frozen in preoccupation with the ugly, violent, and grotesque features of contemporary life to the exclusion of all others.

One thinks especially of those writers whose names may, for the most part, be unfamiliar to the general reading public but who have come to be thought of as forming a new experimental avant-garde, even as being the producers of a "post-contemporary" fiction. They include Jerzy Kosinski and Donald Barthelme (the best known of the group), Robert Coover, Ronald Sukenick, Gilbert Sorrentino, Steve Katz, Richard Brautigan, and some others who publish almost entirely in the more obscure little magazines.

It may be true, as their chief supporter, Jerome Klinkowitz, has argued in his book, *Literary Disruptions*, that these writers have carried fiction away from the dead end of exhaustion where old-fashioned contemporary, John Barth, proclaimed it to be. But what remains to be demonstrated is whether they have carried it in an important new direction and infused it with fresh energy and meaning.

The most troubling feature of this so-called post-contemporary group is essentially a further development of what was troubling about their immediate predecessors who some years ago achieved a certain meretricious popularity for the kind of satire then known as dark comedy or black humor. In too many instances black humor was enfeebled by the fact that it cut itself off from the vital source of effective satire—the close observation of the social and political world—and it evidently did so because it was too easily horrified by the grotesqueness and complexity of that world and found it less painful to retreat into cuteness (as does Kurt Vonnegut) or fabulation (as does Thomas Pynchon) than to endure and create the genuine dark comedy of contemporary experience. The result was that the living reality of the object or condition being satirized was too obliquely suggested in the work of these writers, or was altogether absent.

In the years that have passed since black humor came into fashion and literature has allegedly evolved from the contemporary to the post-contemporary, there has been very little actual change except that the typifying attitudes and artistic devices of black humor have been absorbed into the public domain and become institutionalized there. They now form part of the official convention of negativist discourse through which, not only in fiction but also in poetry, drama, journalism, and film, we habitually register our bafflement or outrage at the insane discontinuities and seemingly gratuitous malevolence of contemporary life. They are available now, like processed food in a supermarket, to any artist or social commentator in need of a jar of pickled *Angst* or instant Doom, and these ingredients had better be abundantly present in any work with pretensions to being taken seriously as an honest statement about the larger unrealities of our time.

But to the extent that the tradition of black humor has led to the substitution of buzz words and stereotypical formulations for fresh imaginative perceptions, it has conditioned the public to respond in certain prescribed ways to experience without really providing them with the experience. If one finds the conditions of contemporary life deranging, one can take comfort from the fact that black humor long ago identified derangement as the only sane response, classified it as the prime symptom of entropy, anomie, atomization, and other derivatives of the second law of thermodynamics, and perfected certain highly stylized modes of dramatizing it in fictional form. Thus, one knows that whenever the characters in a novel do not resemble human beings, it is because they have been dehumanized by the entropic forces that are fast dehumanizing us all. Whenever a fictional landscape seems fragmented or nightmarishly surreal, so that it is impossible to tell what precisely is going on, one knows that it is intended to function as a metaphor of the disorientation of the psyche when confronted with the bizarre arbitrariness of events. If the experiences and people portrayed in a novel seem trivial or empty, one can be sure they seem so because they represent the exhausted sensibility of the age.

In short, the tradition of black humor has provided us with a number of analogical evocations of the psychological disturbances of contemporary life, evocations that are sometimes so compelling we are almost persuaded that they actually do reveal reality rather than merely a set of stock responses to it. Yet over and over again in black humor fiction, as well as in the post-contemporary fiction descending from it, the problem is that although the responses may be powerfully rendered, the concrete events and specific social circumstances that induced them are seldom identified or objectified. That essential dimension of fiction that Hemingway once described as comprising "the exact sequence of motion and fact which made the emotion" is almost always missing, leaving the emotion afloat in a causeless void.

In the fiction of Barthelme, Sukenick, Coover, and some of the other writers discussed by Mr. Klinkowitz, virtually everything and everyone exists in such a radical state of distortion and aberration that there is no way of determining from which conditions in the real world they have been derived or from what standard of sanity they may be said to depart. The conventions of verisimilitude and sanity have been nullified. Characters inhabit a dimension of structureless being in which their behavior becomes inexplicably arbitrary and unjudgeable because the fiction itself stands as a metaphor of a derangement that is seemingly without provocation and beyond measurement.

This may be to suggest that these writers have lost or never possessed an understanding of the real experiences which have provoked their negativist responses, that they have inherited from the modernist past certain attitudes which their classic predecessors did derive from such experiences but which are now activated by unthinking Pavlovian reflex in these writers whenever the impulse arises to write fiction. In short, it would appear that for them the attitudes have become sacred gospel and no longer need to be tested to determine whether they bear any relation to reality. In this respect, Barthelme and the others are like a primitive tribe compulsively carrying on a ritual of self-immolation long after all memory of the perhaps dire necessities that prompted their ancestors to originate it has been lost in the fog of antiquity.

Barthelme, for example, might not unfairly be described as the inheritor of that bleakest and most negative idea of experience patented and perfected by such classic modernists as Beckett and Céline. His point of view is grounded in the *a priori* assumption that the contemporary world consists of nothing but trivia and dreck. A reader of his stories finds himself immersed in a nasty sea of evacuated crud and muck, all the befouled garbage of a disposable-waste culture spreading pollution over every area of human activity. Some of the stories very effectively dramatize the sensations of being shat upon and generally despoiled that accompany so much of the daily experience of contemporary life. Yet, as I have charged elsewhere, they do not dramatize the cultural, political, or historical circumstances that *give rise to* these sensations, nor do they end in a satirical or even a specific thematic formulation. Everything is offered in deadpan and with the mechanical iterativeness of items recited from a grocery list. Everything is offered, but somehow nothing is given.

There is also the problem that a writer holding to the belief that the world consists of nothing but dreck must necessarily work under a grave limitation. His imagination is required to convert everything into terms acceptable to his metaphysics— and like a digestive system it matters not at all what rich variety of substances may enter it. By the time its function is completed, all things come out looking and smelling the same.

In Sukenick's novel called simply *Out* the depicted experience —to the extent that it can be determined—is a collage of the kinds of strained distortion made obligatory by the gospel of the Wasteland outlook. Nothing that may or may not happen in the narrative is what it appears to be or remains for long what it may have begun by being. Characters who are not identified or whose identities change from moment to moment drift in and out of a phantasmagoric journey through an opaque medium in which, by slow degrees, all movement sinks into randomness and all response becomes increasingly attenuated and arbitrary—evidently not in obedience to some sustained vision of entropic collapse such as Pynchon's but as a result of some ultimate exhaustion of mind and spirit, some abdication of vision apparently brought about by Sukenick's discovery that meaning cannot be located and that there is really nothing out there worth the bother of envisioning.

The intention of such an approach is of course to suggest precisely that this is in fact the case: anarchy and arbitrariness have so completely overtaken human affairs that the effort to create or disclose coherence is quite useless; all forms are invalid or illusory; identity is a matter of what one claims or chooses it to be. In short, the novel is a mail-order catalogue of all the fashionable post-contemporary clichés designed to convey the intelligence that nothing is intelligible and that fiction in such a circumstance is not even fictive but just as fictitious as the unreality it cannot even muster the energy to treat effectively.

Behind it all is the equally familiar notion that there exists some universal but unlocatable conspiracy and an inevitable counter-conspiracy, which together are responsible for mystifying all occurrences and making it constantly uncertain whether they in fact are occurring. Arising out of this prepackaged *Weltanschauung*—which in current fiction has clearly become the last metaphysical refuge of imaginations too feeble to function in the face of complexity—is the requirement that characters assume disguises and pseudonyms in place of personalities and that their principal business in the narrative be to change their names as frequently as possible.

Thus, Sukenick's polynomial narrator announces his intention at the beginning of the novel to become not a character but a corrasable label: "Today I'm Harrold. Two r's. Tomorrow I might be someone else." But then we know that according to the orthodoxly negativist vision of contemporary experience, individual identity is just as meaningless as the common everyday occurrences that are of such incredible bizarreness that they cannot be believed or comprehended. Harrold and a girl known for the moment for unknown reasons as President Nixon are making their way along a window ledge seven stories up when they happen to witness just such an occurrence. They reach a window and Harrold winks and motions President Nixon to look inside.

> Inside a blond girl nude to the waist and wearing bobbysox hovers over a scrawny adolescent boy tied to a wooden chair his head hanging like a wilted flower. As they watch she grabs him by the jaws with one hand forcing his mouth open inserts a gleaming knife and severs his tongue. Blood covers his chin the severed tongue bounces off his chest and lands in his lap where it wags horribly several times in a growing pool of blood. Then she takes hold of her breast and shoves it in the boy's mouth which makes sucking motions.
>
> President Nixon looks from the window to Harrold. Is this true she says.

No, it is not, and the scene's grotesque departure from the true tells us nothing about the frequently grotesque nature of the true, a quality that is captured in successful caricature. Nothing in the scene is earned or learned from experience. Its cheap and wholly gratuitous ugliness is not meant to signify but to stupify. And what is being imperfectly concealed is the fact that Sukenick is endeavoring so to derange the reader's sense of the significance and credibility of what is taking place that he will not be able to recognize that nothing of significance is taking place.

Coover's *The Public Burning* perfectly embodies the hysteria behind the simplistic politics of the activist sixties, the literary corollary of which is the simplistic negativism of so much post-contemporary fiction. Like Barthelme and Sukenick, Coover believes that the experience of our time, and particularly American experience, consists of nothing but dreck, and again like them, he appears to have arrived at this conclusion as if it came to him engraved on stone direct from Mount Sinai rather than through a critical assessment of specific conditions leading logically to it. The result is that he lumps together without reason or discrimination many highly dissimilar features and institutions of American life in a splenetic diatribe evidently formed on the premise so coveted by the sixties that all enlightened souls are programmed to despise these things and need not be told precisely what is despicable about them.

Using as the occasion for his attack what is for him the most egregious miscarriage of justice in living memory—the execution of Julius and Ethel Rosenberg for passing atomic secrets to the Russians—Coover composes a preposterous epic-catalogue of culprits responsible for it. They range from Cecil B. DeMille, who stages a massive Hollywood-style extravaganza in Times Square where the Rosenbergs are to be electrocuted before a cheering cast of thousands, to Betty Crocker, who presides over the festivities, and Gene Autry, who will provide vocal accompaniment, while Harry James and His Orchestra play overhead on the Astor Roof. In the audience on Electrocution Night are to be found, in spirit or in flesh, such notables as Dale Carnegie, Ty Cobb, Admiral Halsey, Ezio Pinza, Cole Porter, and Shirley Temple. But, ultimately, just about every prominent national figure and political institution from J. Edgar Hoover and the F.B.I. through the Presidential Cabinet, Supreme Court, and Congress is indicted as an accomplice in the gigantic conspiracy against the sainted Rosenbergs.

Interspersed through the novel are long sections of narrative by then Vice-President Nixon who is quite perceptively characterized in his high-minded malevolence and who is shown to develop a romantic passion for Ethel Rosenberg, which is very nearly consummated, either in masturbatory fantasy or fictional fact, when he visits her in Sing Sing. But it turns out that Nixon is destined to experience a far more excruciating fulfillment. At the end, following the executions, he is cornered inside the belly of a Disneyland whale and massively buggered by Uncle Sam himself, a gargantuan, wise-cracking figure of hayseed nastiness who is evidently supposed to embody Coover's vision of the bottomless depravity of the national spirit. Inevitably, after the initial agony of penetration, Nixon enjoys being raped—a consequence that would not seem to demand heavy explication.

The obvious trouble with the novel—if, in fact, it is a novel—is that in it Coover tells us absolutely nothing about the American political situation at the time of the Rosenberg executions, nor does he illuminate satirically that darkest and most ominous political development of the postwar era, the witchhunt undertaken by Joseph McCarthy and his supporters to combat what they deemed to be a worldwide Communist conspiracy. Instead, Coover makes an indictment, which is quite as pathologically sweeping as any of McCarthy's, of just about everything and everyone popularly associated with the American way of life, and he does so by adopting the kind of shrill sophomoric bombast with which activist leaders used to harangue street crowds during the more violent demonstrations of the sixties. The sickness for him as for them is universal. It infects every fiber of the national character; it is endemic to our national history and our cultural and political life; and it has been intentionally spread through the secret conduits of the conspiracy engineered by the military-industrial complex, which is determined to brainwash an innocent citizenry and conscript it into the service of its nefarious aims.

His comic-book caricature of Uncle Sam is the perfect defining image for Coover's mindless evacuation of spleen and is of course the most familiar kind of caricature in the limited activist repertoire. But Uncle Sam is an image that never achieves the significance of a symbol or parable because the relation between the malignant traits attributed to him and particular symptoms of malignancy in the nation is never dramatized. In fact, nothing in the novel really signifies or connotes because paranoid hallucination and blind fury have wholly disoriented whatever critical perspective Coover may have had. To depict America as a rapacious howling savage may be melodramatic, but it is as preposterous as implicating Betty Crocker in the fate of the Rosenbergs unless the connection is made explicit. By the same token, the evocation of the Waste Land image to represent the sterility of the modern world makes no sense unless the symptoms of sterility are specified. And those who resort automatically to the image—as do Barthelme, Sukenick, and Coover—should be reminded that in the mother poem T.S. Eliot presented a devastating and extremely specifying portrait of both the symptoms and their causes.

This, as I have said, is what finally seems most problematical about the work of many of the so-called post-contemporary

writers: that their negativist vision of reality has become auto-
mated to the point where they seem no longer to know, if they
ever knew, from exactly what specific circumstances it has been
derived. The horror or contempt their fiction characteristically
expresses is far in excess of the facts they are able to marshal in
its support. It is as if their classification as post-contemporary
suggested not so much that they possess a deeper or more
prophetic understanding of current realities than that enjoyed
by their now antiquated fellow writers but rather that they have
left the contemporary world so far behind that they can no
longer conceive it imaginatively or present it in terms more
definite than a vague and disembodied attitude of total disdain.
Hence, so much of their work tends to have the quality of an
unfocused raging against an empty landscape or a mirror held
up in anger to a void.

By contrast, some of the merely contemporary writers such as
Heller, Bellow, and Gaddis appear to possess sufficient imagination and moral sensitivity to understand not only that the void
exists but from just what standards of order, reason, and
humanity we have fallen in the process of entering it.

Behind the comic absurdities in Heller's fiction, for example,
one can perceive the actualities of the observable world his
comedy exaggerates. His characters are almost always grotesques,
but they are *presented* as grotesques, and with no suggestion that
grotesqueness is the natural and universal state of being. One is
always certain, furthermore, precisely to what degree they and
their situation are absurd or insane, because his narrative point
of view is located in an observer with whom we can identify—
as is the case with both Yossarian in *Catch-22* and Bob Slocum
in *Something Happened*—and who is just rational enough to be
able to measure the departures from rationality in the people and
situations he encounters.

Yossarian's problem is that he is hopelessly sane in a situation
of complete madness. The high comedy of the novel is generated
by the fact that military life, when viewed satirically—which is
to say, rationally—becomes ludicrous and, in wartime, malevolent.
But there is nothing in *Catch-22* that a person of Yossarian's
perpetually affronted sensibility would not have perceived in

the same circumstances. The boundaries of the normal and predictable are never exceeded, but they are extended satirically to the point where, as happens in wars, all kinds of idiocy, cruelty, obsessive self-interest, and the most inhumane bureaucratic exploitation are made to seem normal and predictable, hence altogether horrifying. The big joke of the "catch" itself—that the men cannot be grounded for reasons of insanity because they are sane enough not to want to fly the required missions—is a particularly sick joke because it might so easily have been a reality. Colonel Scheisskopf, who ponders various ways in which his men might be wired or nailed together in order to produce a perfect marching pattern; the general who orders his squadrons to bomb a village that has no strategic significance whatever because he wants photographs showing a perfect bombing pattern; Milo Minderbinder, who creates a massive syndicate involved in the exchange and sale of goods to both the Allies and the Axis powers, and who for a fee will arrange the bombing of his own men; Doc Daneeka, who, because he was scheduled to be aboard a plane that crashed, is declared officially dead, even though he is standing there protesting that he is alive—all are cartoon figures made plausible because they are extensions of the cold logic of wartime insanity. But in their comic extravagance these characters and others serve to dramatize Heller's altogether uncomic hatred of a system, supposedly consecrated to high patriotic service, that could so easily become diabolical because it views people as inanimate objects to be manipulated and destroyed for inane reasons. In such a situation Yossarian clearly has abundant provocations for his paranoia. There are real enemies out there, whether on our side or theirs, and, as he repeatedly complains, they are trying to kill him. But the vastly more frightening concern is that if he has no identity as a human being, then his death will have no significance—a concern that writers like Barthelme, Sukenick, and Coover, in their creation of characters who have little or no significance, appear not to share.

In Bellow also the departures from reason or humanity that his fiction records can be evaluated and understood because, like Heller, he makes use again and again of highly sensitive monitory characters such as Herzog, Mr. Sammler, and Charles Citrine who become the suffering victims of these departures and sustain a perspective of insulted sanity that contains Bellow's own moral perspective on the erosion of rational and civilized values in the contemporary world.

Gaddis's moral perspective in *JR* is expressed implicitly in the whole enormously complex fabric of the narrative. The breakdown of the communicative power of language is dramatized through specific illustrations of the atrocities of computer jargon and bureaucratese, and as the action proceeds to disintegrate into ever more extravagant extremes of incoherence, one is kept always reminded of the degree of the extravagance by Gaddis's unwavering sense of what is humanly tolerable and reasonable, by what I have called the conserving and correcting power of his imagination.

Although for historical reasons it is displayed in rather different terms, a comparable vision of values maligned or betrayed underlies the work of some of the most important classic modernists and helps to prevent their imaginative portraits of moral decay from becoming as empty of meaning as the experiences from which the portraits derive. One thinks again of *The Waste Land* in which twentieth-century culture is presented as disintegrated in a poetry so fragmented and dissonant that it seems the perfect verbal embodiment of its subject. Yet, finally, the effect of disintegration is absorbed into a structure of new or salvaged order, and the "fragments shored against my ruin" by the protagonist at the end are also shored against both the ruinous demise of the poem in chaos and the ruin of the modern age in moral anarchy—the shoring force becoming by the end a massive unifying conception of human history and the world's religions.

There is a strikingly similar effect in Joyce's *Ulysses* in which modern existence is shown to be randomly entropic, yet where, after being presented as shifting proteanly through the seemingly arbitrary perspectives of the narrative, it is given the ultimate form, not merely of Joyce's wonderfully cohering art, but of harmonic relationship with the fundamental rhythms of all life and history. Molly Bloom's ecstatically reiterated "yes" in her closing monologue affirms more than the robust sexuality of her relation to life. It is also Joyce's celebration of his belief in the existence of a vital principle of orderly growth underlying the apparently purposeless flux and flow of the experiences his novel so complexly records.

The American literary generation slightly younger than Eliot and Joyce were endowed by history with a unique perspective, which became for some of them an important basis for imaginative moral judgment. They began their careers when the fundamental experiences of the modern age were just becoming visible in their full difference from those of the past and when the methods for dramatizing them in literary form were in the process of being perfected. They were thus privileged to make formulations of the most primary and innovative kind about the nature of the new era that was fast evolving around them—in effect, to complete the work of establishing the basic premises of modern American literature. If, as many commentators have observed, World War I had left them with an abiding distrust of official values as well as a feeling of dislocation from the past, they were also, in an important sense, purged of illusion and freed to define their postwar perspective in relation to the best that might be reclaimed from the past. Their profound need for moral and emotional authenticity, to find a way to recognize and express the exact truth of their own perceptions, led them to make a skeptical and, in many instances, satirical scrutiny of the changes in American life that had begun to occur with such rapidity after the war. And not at all surprisingly, they often came to examine the new manners and morals by comparing them with those that had so recently become outmoded. It was as if by trying to determine the current validity of what had gone into the discard, they might penetrate the meaning of what had come into being.

Clearly, they were creatively stimulated by the experience of living in a dramatic, changing present, but they could also feel anxious and uncertain and in need of the structures of coherence and identity they had known in the Midwest or the South. This perhaps accounts for the fact that Hemingway and Fitzgerald were so continuously preoccupied with procedural questions, with the effort to formulate dependable rules of feeling and conduct. Hemingway's works can be read as a series of instruction manuals on how to respond to and comport one's self in the testing situations of life now that the rules have changed. It might also be argued that some of his most dependable instructions are those he was able to reclaim from the past, in particular the American frontier past, the lessons of courage, fidelity, and honor that might still have the power to influence human conduct when all other values were being called into question. Fitzgerald's best novels are restatements of Henry James's great theme: the implications of the misuse of power over those who are innocent and helpless by those who are strong and unscrupulous.

In short, one finds in these writers and in some of their contemporaries a concern with the moral authenticity of certain traditions they might have presumed to be outmoded. It may be expressed only in a nostalgic recurrence to the locales that provided security in childhood—Hemingway's Big Two-Hearted River, Faulkner's South, or Thomas Wolfe's Old Catawba. But it may also involve complex loyalties and codes of honor that once gave a human dimension to life—as Nick Carraway discovers through the experience of Gatsby, and Dick Diver through his marriage to Nicole. Both characters derived a "sense of the fundamental decencies" from their fathers and so can evaluate and condemn a society in which such decencies no longer have meaning.

One of the very best of Fitzgerald's stories, "Babylon Revisited," is yet another expression of the desire to reconstitute certain values of moral discipline and self-control after the violent dissipations of the decade that ended in bankruptcy in 1929. Charlie Wales, a battered survivor of the time, returns to Paris in the hope of regaining custody of his daughter. To do this he must prove to his sister-in-law that he has become a fit and responsible person. He very nearly succeeds in convincing her, but fails at the last moment when two of his old drinking friends reappear and destroy his chances of making a new life. Just as Nick after Gatsby's death wanted "the world to be in uniform and at a sort of moral attention forever," so Charlie felt the need "to jump back a whole generation and trust in character

again as the eternally valuable element." But there is no escape
from the consequences of his wasted past:

> Again the memory of those days swept over him like a
> nightmare—the people they had met traveling: then people
> who couldn't add a row of figures or speak a coherent
> sentence . . . the women and girls carried screaming with
> drink or drugs out of public places.
> —The men who locked their wives out in the snow, because
> the snow of twenty-nine wasn't real snow. If you didn't want
> it to be snow, you just paid some money.

For some of the American writers who immediately preceded
Hemingway and Fitzgerald—and I think particularly of H.L.
Mencken, Sinclair Lewis, and Sherwood Anderson—the basis for
a critical judgment of the national life derived not from an act
of attempted moral reclamation, but rather from a vehement
repudiation of some of the same values, which, ironically, their
successors sought to reclaim. Where Hemingway and Fitzgerald
looked back with some nostalgia and more than a little romantic
illusion to a time when certain provincial standards of decency
and honor seemed to make possible the virtuous life, the
Mencken generation viewed the values of American provincial
culture from the more sophisticated perspective of the urban
East and Europe, and they found them so impoverished and
banal that they could not conceivably support a civilized life of
whatever degree of virtue.

To a far greater extent than Hemingway and Fitzgerald, some
of the older writers like Anderson and Lewis had had very direct
experience of the conditions of life in the towns and cities of
the Midwest, and they had suffered personally from the hostility
to artistic culture and ideas, the fear of emotion, the sexual
hypocrisy, the sterility of the physical landscape, the Babbittry
and Boosterism that seemed to them to typify the real Wines-
burgs, Zeniths, and Gopher Prairies in which they grew up and
about which they later came to write.

This is to suggest that unlike so many writers of the present
time they had been able to have a vital relationship with the
concrete objects of their rebellion against American life, even

if it was a deeply traumatic relationship, even if their involvement with that life was the result of the very intensity of their
estrangement from it. But it is becoming more and more evident
that there are kinds and qualities of estrangement, of which some
are creatively invigorating and others stultifying. So long as
writers believe—as did Mencken and his contemporaries—that
they are the chief custodians of sanity and civilization, they will
be able to attack their society for failing to be sane and civilized,
and they will be able to do this even more effectively just because
they feel estranged from their society. But if writers feel—as
many now seem to do—so completely estranged that they can
perceive their society only as a nightmare aberration, a condition
of malevolent conspiracy, or a mass of undifferentiated human-
oids, then obviously they will not be able to engage it imaginatively with very much vigor or profundity. The essential
connection will have been broken—or never have been forged—
that might have made it possible for them to assume a meaningful critical stance, and the perspective will be lost or never
gained that might have made effective satire possible. For the
basis of effective satire is a clear perception of the specific
conditions that need to be critically examined as well as a clear
knowledge of the standards of reason and humanity which those
conditions violate and, in the violation, become preposterous.

CHAPTER XI

Jogging Towards Bethlehem

*If you do away with this (intense spiritual struggle) and
maintain that by tolerance, benevolence, inoffensiveness, and
a redistribution or increase of purchasing power . . . the
world will be as good as anyone could require, then you must
expect human beings to become more and more vaporous.*

T.S. Eliot

In considering the imaginative situation of American writers at
the present time one cannot avoid the impression that the events
and metaphysical climate of the past two decades have had a
decidedly debilitating effect on their ability to achieve a critical
or satirical perspective on their society. Ten years ago I made
the observation that our writers were unable to evaluate critically
the youth culture of the sixties because they could no longer be
certain that not only they but others like them, the members of
the literary and intellectual establishment, were still the chief
custodians of sanity and civilization, or would be in agreement
with them as to what those terms meant in relation to the youth
culture.

The passage may be worth quoting in full:

> Such men as Lewis and Mencken were the spokesmen in
> their day for a minority of enlightened people who did
> generally share such agreement, and who also shared certain

common attitudes toward American society. Theirs was, like ours, an age of social revolution and social criticism. But the principal target of criticism was the way of life and thinking of the unenlightened majority, the vast population we now call Middle America. The issues in dispute must seem to us very simple and even rather naive. The conflict was largely between truth and hypocrisy, freedom against repression, liberalism against prejudice, cosmopolitanism against provincialism. The intellectuals who were crusading for truth and freedom clearly had *right* on their side. Civilization was waging and finally winning the war against barbarism.

But the interesting fact about the present time is that the most powerfully evident cultural influence is no longer that of provincial and small-town America. We know that America still exists, but it no longer creates the prevailing ideological climate of the country. Today we live in a climate of political activism and moral idealism generated in large part by the youth movement with the encouragement of significant elements of the adult intellectual community. It would seem, on the face of it, that the youth movement may be, and ought to be, as vulnerable to criticism and satire as the provincial culture of Lewis's and Mencken's day. In fact, there is more than a little justice in the charge that the youth culture has become the influential and conformist society at this time, that it constitutes a sort of new Babbittry or *Booboisie* of the left, and that it is characterized by as much self-righteousness, smugness, humorlessness, and generalized sentimentality and vapidity as could ever have been encountered fifty years ago on the streets of Gopher Prairie. Furthermore, many of the social attitudes and life styles of the youth culture are just as dictatorial and repressive of individuality as the most authoritarian codes of the old middle-class establishment.

But the very great difference is that where Mencken and Lewis knew that they represented, and were speaking for, enlightened opinion, the youth culture seems to have very nearly all the weight of enlightened opinion on its side. Many intellectuals and others who would normally be champions of civilized values have closed down their critical faculties with regard to much that the young stand for, because they are so impressed by the idealism of the young and by the indisputable moral rightness of many of their social aims. Hence, the writer who would attempt to criticize or satirize some of the reprehensible, or just plain ridiculous, features of the youth culture would almost inevitably find himself categorized as a reactionary or even a Fascist, an apologist for the establishment, and relegated to the company of many people whose social and political philosophy he would undoubtedly find abhorrent in the extreme. In other words, he would not be able to write honestly about many vulnerable characteristics of the young without seeming to provide ammunition to the enemy, and to *his* enemy, without violating some of his own liberal-humanitarian convictions. By a nicely ironic turning of the tables, the subversive critical opinion is now the unenlightened reactionary opinion, while the enlightened opinion is the liberal conformist opinion.

There is also the difficulty that satire is most effectively written about hypocrisy and the effort of an entrenched society to preserve appearances by lying about its behavior and its real motives. Usually, satire exposes the disparity between appearances and reality, between humanitarian or libertarian professions and self-seeking actions, between snobbery about material values and pretensions about moral or spiritual values. Now clearly there are elements in the youth movement that are open to satire on these grounds. There is snobbery. There is pretentiousness. There may even be hypocrisy about the real self-seeking motives behind the movement.

But again the difference is that the young have right and righteousness, at least in principle, on their side. They are not calling for the preservation of outmoded institutions, but just the opposite. They are not calling for repression—even if they are themselves sometimes repressive. They are calling for freedom. It would at least appear that they are not materialistic but militantly anti-materialistic. There may be much insufferable pietism connected with their position, but so much of it is morally unimpeachable that to satirize it would be to impugn the good principles on which it is based. Hence, the impulse to satirize must inevitably be short-circuited, and the writer loses one of his most important freedoms: the freedom to pronounce upon the condition of his society according to the honesty of his vision.

One might well look back with some nostalgia to the era and the conditions described in that passage. For one thing, the pieties urged upon us by the youth culture of the sixties were at least urged with some vigor and drama. But by a process of fairly rapid evolution from heretical sanctimony to canonical cliché, the pieties of the sixties have become the unchallengeable dogmas of the eighties, so taken for granted by the society at large that discussion of them has virtually ceased because there exists no adversary position from which their sovereignty might be questioned, hence, no enlightened point of view from which their absurdity might be criticized or satirized by our writers. We have, in fact, progressed about as far along the way as seems humanly possible toward the egalitarian society that was a central dream of the sixties and that is now well past the verge of becoming a dreary but altogether sacrosanct reality. No dissenting voice can sensibly be raised against it, since it is being achieved, dreary or not, in accordance with the holiest principles of American democracy. Qualitative distinctions among people or conditions cannot be drawn because not only all men and women but all things that exist are deemed, by virtue of their sheer existence, to be created equal; therefore, no principle or standard of discrimination can be imposed upon them.

It follows logically from this that rampant mediocrity has become a major characterizing feature of our time. No barriers based upon distinction of mind, talent, or character must be erected against the inalienable right of just anyone to do any-thing he chooses to do, without regard for his ability to do it well. Blacks, Chicanos, Navajo Indians, paraplegics, defrocked lesbian nuns from Idaho, and other homosexuals from anywhere must all be accommodated regardless of their qualifications because they belong to a repressed and beleaguered minority collective, and membership in a minority collective carries with it the proviso that the only qualification a member need possess is his membership. As a result, standards of performance in the professional and political areas of the national life have been compromised to the point where we accept it as perfectly natural that people with minimal intelligence and an advanced degree from some reputable institution where for years no grade lower than B has been given to anyone endowed with a warm body and the tuition fee, will be treated as expert authorities in

professional fields that not so very long ago demanded excep-
tional promise and mentality as requirements just for admission
to apprenticeship. In television we are regularly subjected to
talk shows on which the most ordinary and inarticulate people
are invited to give their utterly banal opinions on some of the
most pressing issues of the day, and we have witnessed the ascent
to the Presidency of two quite mediocre men, one a redneck
peanut farmer from Georgia evidently elected on the strength
of his simple-minded religiosity, the other a former minor movie
actor and jellybean addict evidently elected because a sufficient
number of the voting public remembered having seen his face
in films.

One serious result of the mandatory egalitarianism now prevailing among us is that whole areas of the national psyche have
been short-circuited by it and in one way or another depleted of
vital force. To the extent that certain righteous moral imperatives are made to govern the ways in which people are supposed
to think and feel about the conditions of their social environment, and to the further extent that people are persuaded that
contrary ways of thinking and feeling are subversive of the good
and true, an opaque curtain will be drawn between their innate
sense of reality and what they perceive, however dimly, to be
the unreality of their environment. If they feel that they are
permitted to respond only in certain approved ways, then they
will inhibit or repress disapproved responses such as natural
competitiveness, snobbery, or hostility and either take to violence,
sink into apathy, or escape into a protective preoccupation with
the self. Since the environment cannot be authentically engaged,
the self becomes its own environment and sole source of
authenticity, while all else becomes abstract and alien.

I have written at some length about the various ways in which
self-preoccupation resulting from the loss of a sense of personal
connection with the environment has become a dominant subject
matter of our contemporary fiction. But fiction has only given
imaginative form to what has become the dominant condition of
contemporary American life, the symptoms of which are visible
everywhere but perhaps with the greatest clarity in the two most
populous precincts of the national neurosis: our twin obsessions

with physical health and with death—twin because, although seemingly contradictory, they are in fact closely complementary.

It may be commonplace to observe that preoccupation with dying results from a suspicion that one is not and has not been living. And the same might be said about preoccupation with the state of one's physical health. It is when the experience of life ceases to be challenging and adventurous and fails to occupy one's full attention that one begins to be concerned about its inevitable termination in death as well as about the condition of the organism whose efficient functioning is alone capable of postponing the onset of death. After all, there may be something amiss with the muscle tone or the coronary arteries that is causing this feeling that all is not well with the world, that life has lost its flavor and direction, along with the consequent feeling of generalized frustration and malaise. Presumably Henry James knew what he had in mind when, in *The Ambassadors*, he has Lambert Strether beseech Little Bilham to "live all you can; it's a mistake not to. It doesn't so much matter what you do in particular, so long as you have your life. If you haven't had that, what *have* you had?" But now the suspicion weighs heavily upon us that not only do we no longer understand what it means to live all you can, we no longer know whether we are having our lives or how to go about having them or what to do if we discover that we are not having them.

Through a process partly of systematic demythification and partly of natural attrition, we have become dissociated from many of the beliefs and psychological connections that might once have enabled us to answer these questions. We have abolished the concept of an afterlife. The shrinkages of history and territory have forced us to put aside the dream of secular transformation wherein one was able always to pull up stakes and move on to a frontier of fresh challenge and new becoming or, as was the case with James, to possess life fully through deep immersion in the sacramental waters of the actual, the dream that with the Renaissance began to reconstitute the psychic vitality of Western Europe and that made the utopian ideal of the New World both a visionary promise and an apparently attainable practical goal. We have witnessed in our own time a profound disillusionment with the values of personal aspiration and the possibilities of material improvement, a perhaps worldwide narrowing of expectations in virtually all categories of human endeavor. One senses everywhere a recognition that the age as a whole has run through its emotional and spiritual capital, that the various modes of life alternative to our present one have all been tried or are not worth trying, that tomorrow and tomorrow will be no better than or different from the seemingly endless and pointless today.

It is not remarkable, therefore, that we should now inhabit a culture distinguished by its lack of a sense of present purpose and future direction, by a political doctrine based on a worship of the ordinary and a fear of excellence, and by the magnitude of its obsession with mortality. If all one can hope to experience is one's physical life up to the moment it is ended in death, then one's overriding concern is to preserve the state of life, however unrewarding it may be, for as long as possible and to seek distraction from the prospect of death as best one can.

The two attitudes—the suspicion that life has become empty of meaning and the desire nevertheless to avoid confronting its meaningless end in death—are well dramatized in our tendency to subject to morbid pseudo-scientific scrutiny all the conditions and actions of existence, whether they be sex, personal relations, old age, how to win and maintain power over others, or how to watch a loved one die of cancer without feeling anything at all. It is a tendency stemming either from the belief that life is so terrible that to be endured it must be distanced from the personal through the vocabulary of behavioral phenomena—the bloodless language of the computer and the laboratory—or that it is so trivial and insignificant that it needs the rhetorical inflation of being described as a science. Old age and death, for example, have become subjects one takes courses in because they have lost the meaning once given them by community and religion and because taking courses in them is a way of denying their reality. The achievement of an A in a course on death must be an indication that one has mastered and so, by implication, has triumphed over the subject matter. If life is a problem to be solved, then death, the inescapable solution, is a problem to be defused of the problematical, so that one will be able to live without dread with the fact of death in the same way that one lives without joy with the experience of life.

Psychiatry of course is our more openly benevolent form of scientific scrutiny, a creator rather than a destroyer of mystery, a way of remythifying what has elsewhere been demythified. Over most of the century we have looked to it to give us back our sense of wonder over the most delicious and worst-kept secret of all, the nature of ourselves, who are we *really*, and what is the true, albeit hidden meaning of what has happened to us in our lives. Psychiatry long ago took over the function of that part of our minds that once dealt directly with experience simply by confronting and coping with it and, in the process, gave us a sense of the concrete dramatic relation existing between the self and the environment. When that relation began to be disrupted, we began to need help in discovering who we are, and psychiatry supplied it by replacing our atrophied powers of self-understanding with its omniscient technology and focusing our attention on the only environment we had left to confront, ourselves alone in limbo with our fascinating fantasies.

On a more profound level of crassness, television and the many films manufactured solely to induce terror have become another kind of substitute source for mystery and adventurous engagement, and they have done so by providing an external, albeit fictitious object for the fantasies psychiatry has directed toward the beloved subject of ourselves. Simply by changing television channels or attending fright movies we are able to experience contingency and achieve adrenal alert without of course experiencing actual risk. We can enter vicariously into a wide range of ghastly and perilous possibilities, most of them involving a regressive journey backward in human time to a savage ancestral environment teeming with delicious threats of murder and mayhem, and for a little while we have restored the vital connection between ourselves and a reality exterior to and beyond the control and comprehension of ourselves. If most of us are afflicted with the Bob Slocum syndrome, so sensitively diagnosed by Joseph Heller, and inhabit an environment too bland and benevolent to be either confronted or defied, then how restorative to the Idic tissues it is to be transported imaginatively to a world in which enemies are real and ferocious and we are forced to cope once again with the fundamental exigencies of survival.

It matters not at all that the raw materials of mass media drama are derived mostly from the urban ghetto environment of the present time. For the majority of the audience, that environment might as well have existed ten thousand years ago, and its great appeal is that it jolts us out of our psychic sleep with the electrifying reminder, brought up out of the swampy depths of primal memory, that there might, after all, have once been something genuine and menacing outside the solipsistic bubble in which the unrealities of contemporary life have obliged us to become enclosed.

In view of this, it might be said that the currently ubiquitous figure of the jogger is the perfect emblematic image of our age, the supreme embodiment in physical terms of the imperious self-absorption with which, in technological terms, psychiatry has so thoroughly indoctrinated us. The jogger, alone in limbo not with his fantasies but with his precious physique, oblivious of his surroundings, attentive only to the workings of his biological machine, sweating and straining to create through the maximum enhancement of his strength a vitality he cannot discover in the experience of his time—no rough beast its hour come round at last, but an ordinary obsessive soul jogging toward the Bethlehem of his dream of immortality, running to prolong a life into which he might well fear that he will not be born before he dies, that his hour will never come round at last or at all.

Surely, in such pathos some revelation for the novelist is at hand, an abundance of potential material for satire and caricature, lampoon and hilarity, even if one allows for the fact that so much of the absurd pretentiousness of our current way of life is protected from scrutiny because, like the pieties of the sixties, it derives from such morally excellent intentions. The jogger, we are forced to remember, is ostensibly jogging in pursuit of his health, and the pursuit of health is an unassailable *good*, somewhat holier today and far more likely to be profitable than the pursuit of happiness. But ours is a sober, solemn, worried, harried, and hurried time, and we no longer seem able to examine what we think or feel very closely for fear perhaps that we will find ourselves staring into the abyss. And even at our most banal and outlandish we are so troubled and desperate that any attempt at honest analysis would seem like a barbarous invasion of the temple of eternal mourning. Then there is the further problem that the particular symptoms and causes of our manifold disorders are so very difficult to define. That is undoubtedly why so many of our novelists have retreated into fabulation or have tried to dramatize their unspecifiable sense of entropy through the hallucinations of the surreal or have given up the effort of understanding and simply consigned all contemporary experience to the communal dumpheap of the Waste Land outlook.

But perhaps these evasions and prevarications only serve to make the point that the task of imaginatively possessing and expressing the quality of American life has become steadily more complex and may never before have been so complex as it is today, particularly when one considers that the totems and taboos of the culture have become almost impregnably embedded in foundations hardened by the salts of our deepest anxiety. It is possible that the amount of freedom most people and most writers feel is at their disposal is just enough to get them somehow through each day without creating any disturbance or giving someone cause to take offense. There may be no freedom left over for the imagination to do its proper work and no vitality of heart or mind that is not consumed in nervous self-preoccupation. Yet the proper work of the imagination remains to be done and where our novelists are concerned its ultimate objective is clear: to become genuinely and radically subversive once again, to resume the traditional function of examining with the clear eye of sanity whatever are the shams and delusions of the prevailing culture, and, by so doing, to restore some measure of wisdom, wonder, and even delight to the short somber passage of our history through time.

Index